Adult Coloring Series

People Dreams #5

Beauty by Design

Every Face a Story

by
KerryDean

Released for sale
in support of the RocketHub Project:
http://bit.ly/1HCuLk9

We *APPRECIATE* your creations,
and Want to **Show Them**
from the Online Mountain Tops!
Attach a scan of your favorite and email to:

Info@**TeamWorx-Inc**.com

A sense of humility requires us to refrain
from trumpeting our perfection, so
IF you have any feedback, criticism or praise
to share, simply let us know at:
Info@TeamWorx-Inc.com

And IF IF IF you don't like this coloring book,
we'll quickly refund your fee.
Just email us at guarantee@TeamWorx-Inc.com

These were all drawn from life, between 1985 and 1990; in Pattaya and Bangkok, Thailand, during the artist's Toulouse Lautrec phase.

NO PROMOTIONAL PAYMENTS of any sort were made, offered or solicited for the mentions in this. If they're still in business, more power to them.

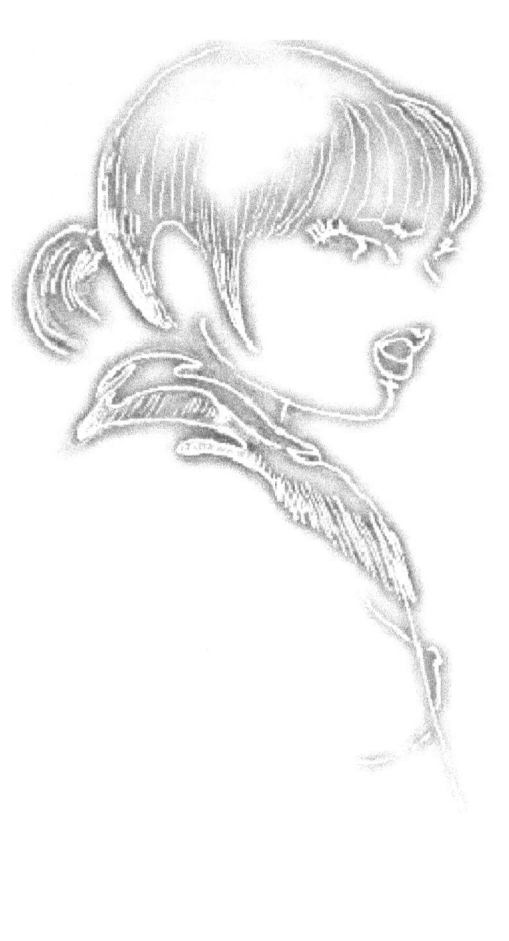

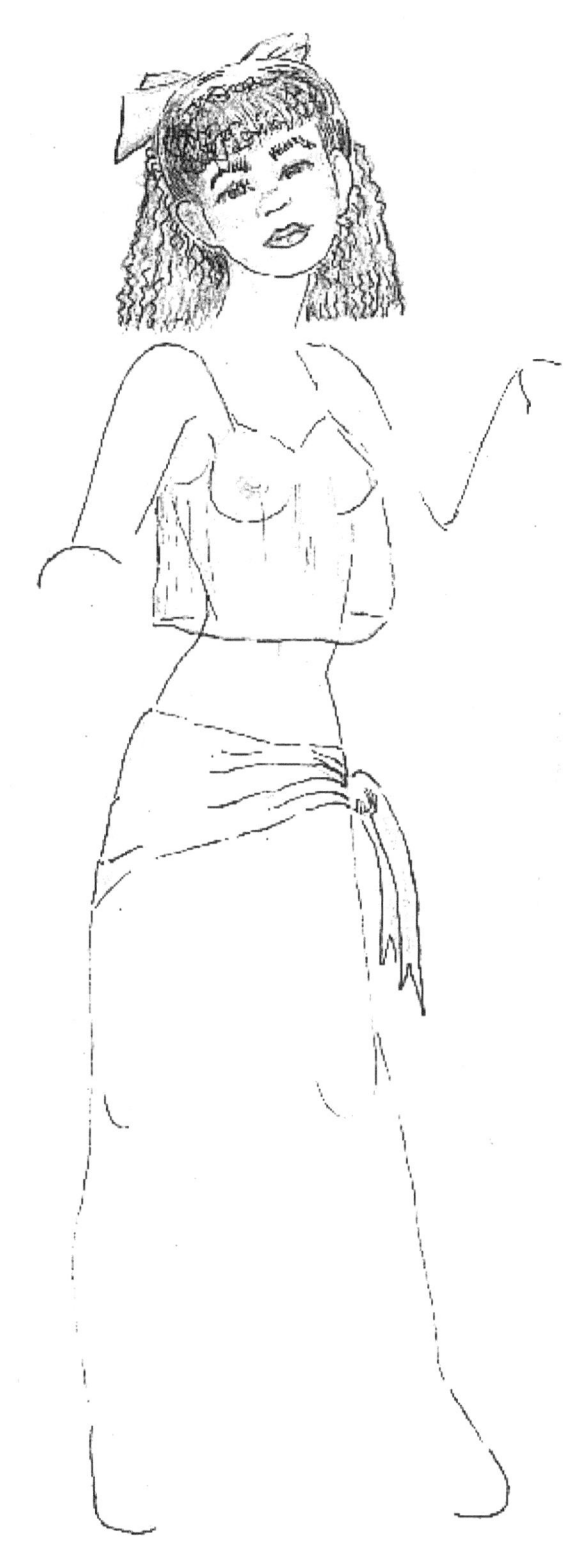

Miss Apple
Miss Apple was a teen-age dancer
at the world-famous 'Baby GoGo'
in Pattaya.
Only 18 at the time of her demise,
she was a flower of radiant
but short bloom...

This is what you get, and all the rest here are UNCOLORED,
just waiting for YOUR artistic touch to fill in color and details.
(Then see Appendix for some stories behind the faces.)

A 12-year-old Baha'i from the islands off the east coast of Thailand. Light-black hair with brown tints, serious eyes and a gentle smile. Okay, and a light-blue shirt, but that hardly matters!

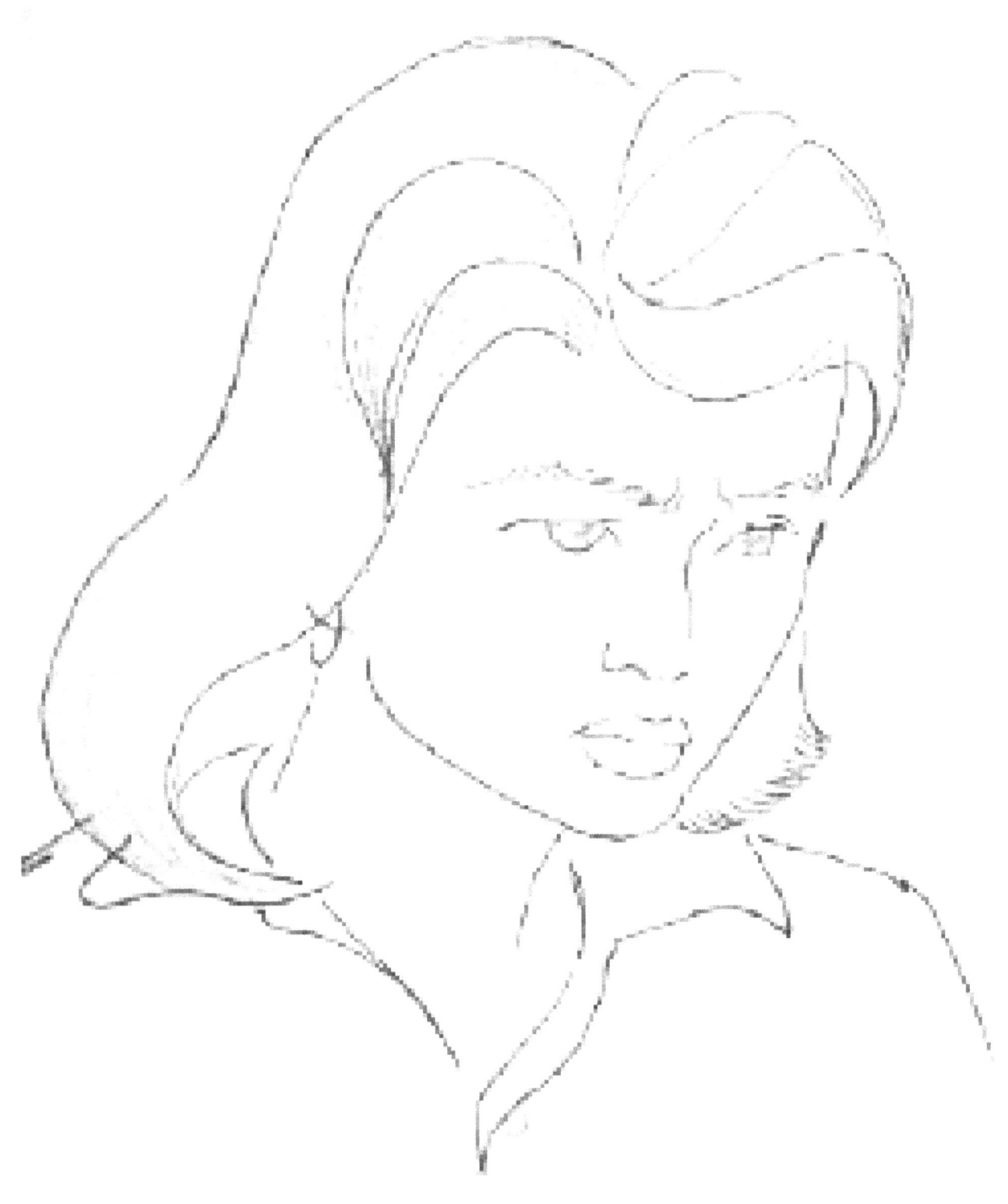

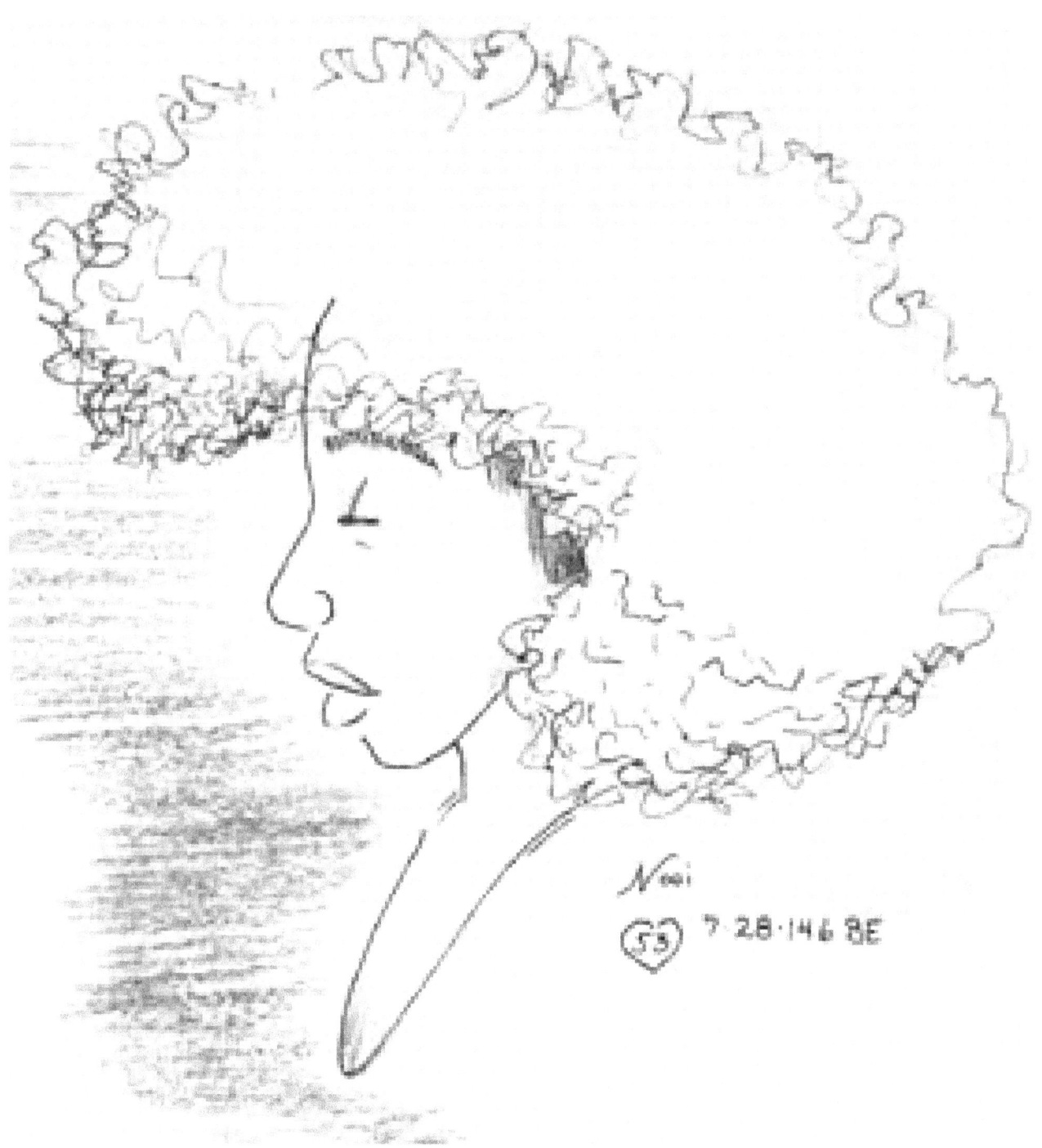

Selected for their elegant design or simplicity of execution,
these drawings were close enough to reality that the subjects
would almost always autograph their sketch.
(Only Mel Gibson wouldn't, but that's a different book...)
This girl showed negroid characteristics in her
lovely, graceful lines.

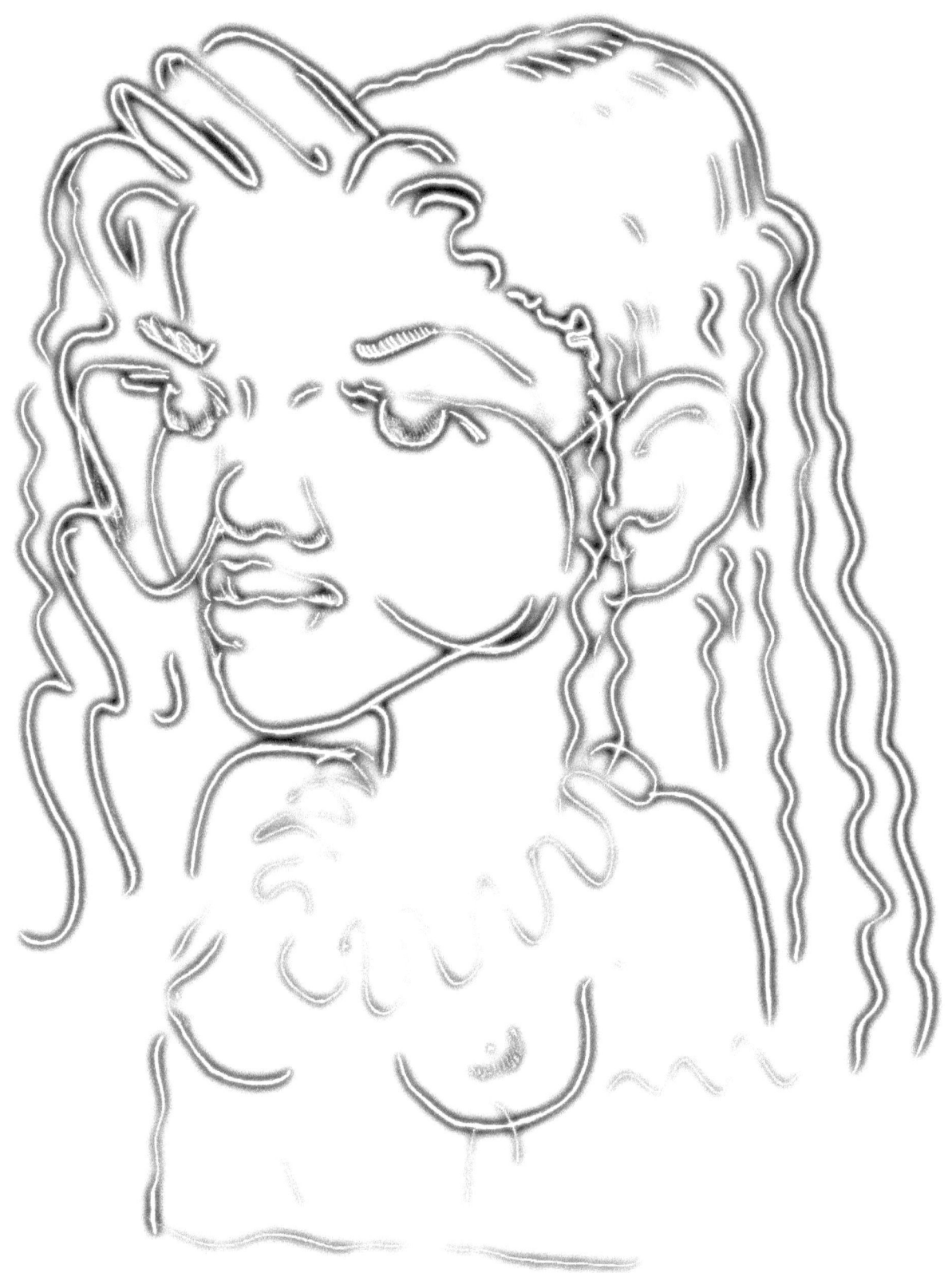

And one from Annie's... yes, her glasses WERE that big!
I would avoid Annie's Soapy Massage, Soi Nana in Bangkok
if I were you...

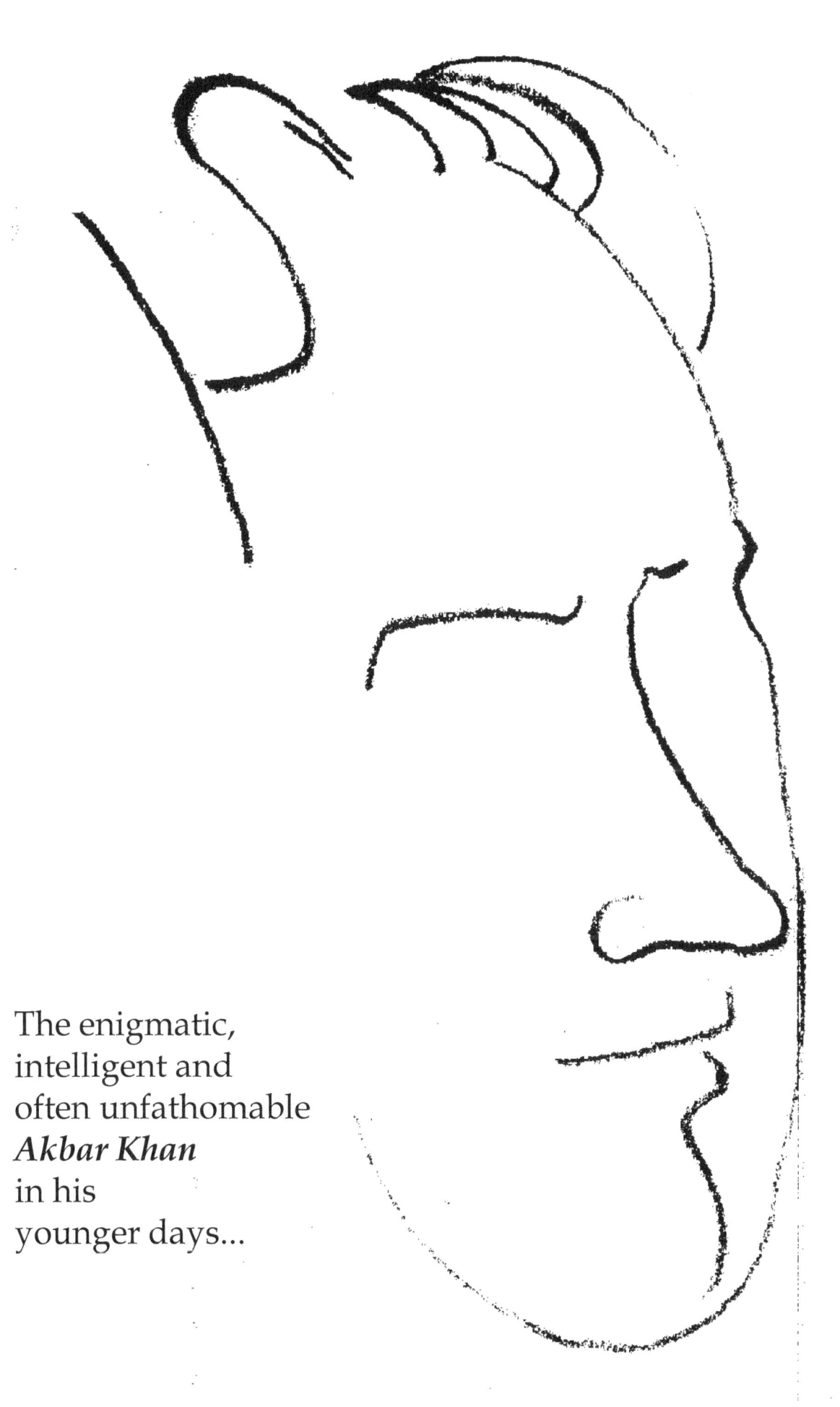

The enigmatic,
intelligent and
often unfathomable
Akbar Khan
in his
younger days...

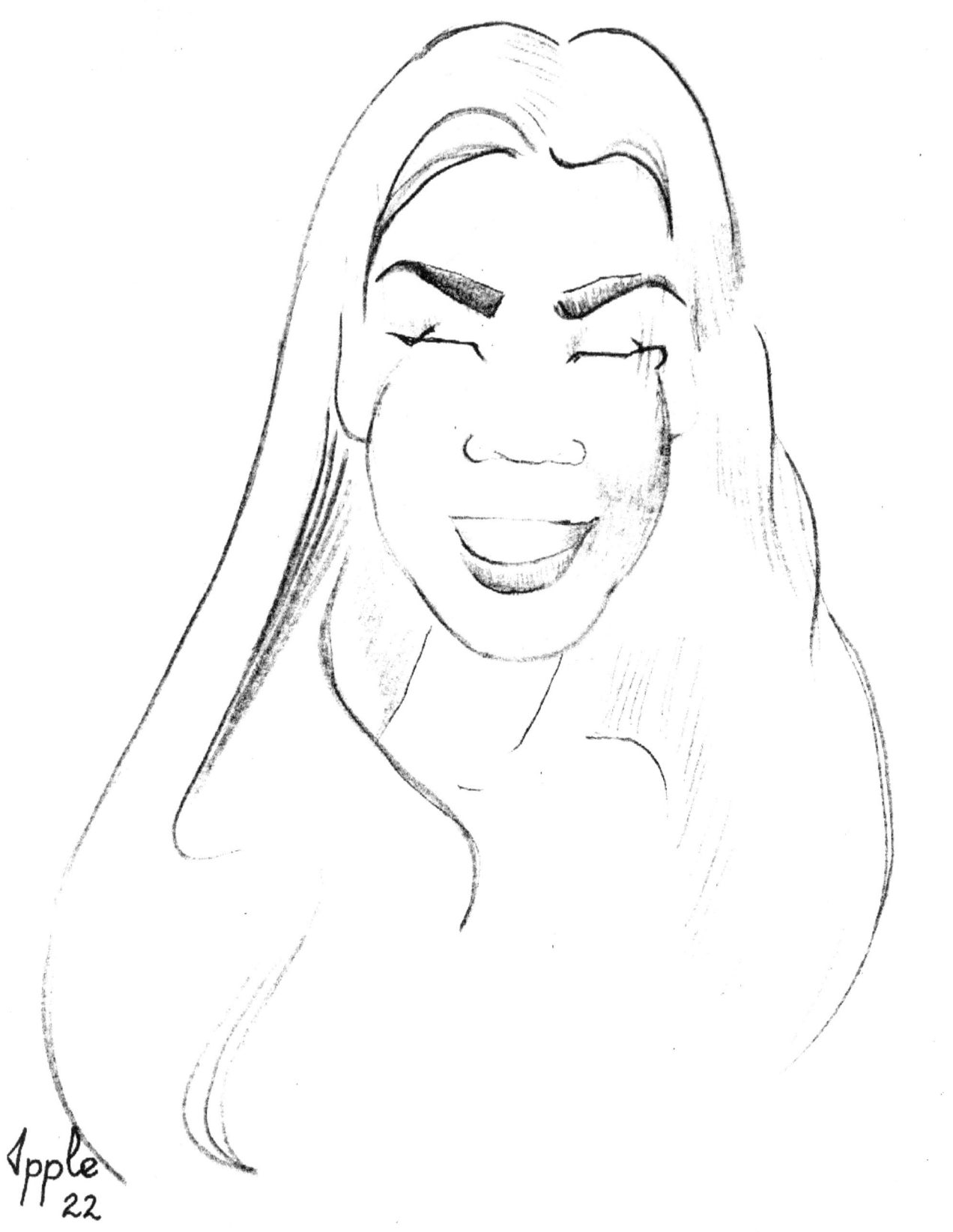

Most Thai women use a nickname rather than their given names, and '*Apple*'
is a fairly common one, although Thais pronounce it '*Appun*'
This Apple was a waitress at a restaurant between South Pattaya and Jomtien.

From Pattaya's most 'successful' lip-synch Cabaret, Simon Cabaret, here's Miss Gaeow. Color the outfit 'Mardi Gras' or Brazilian Float colorful.

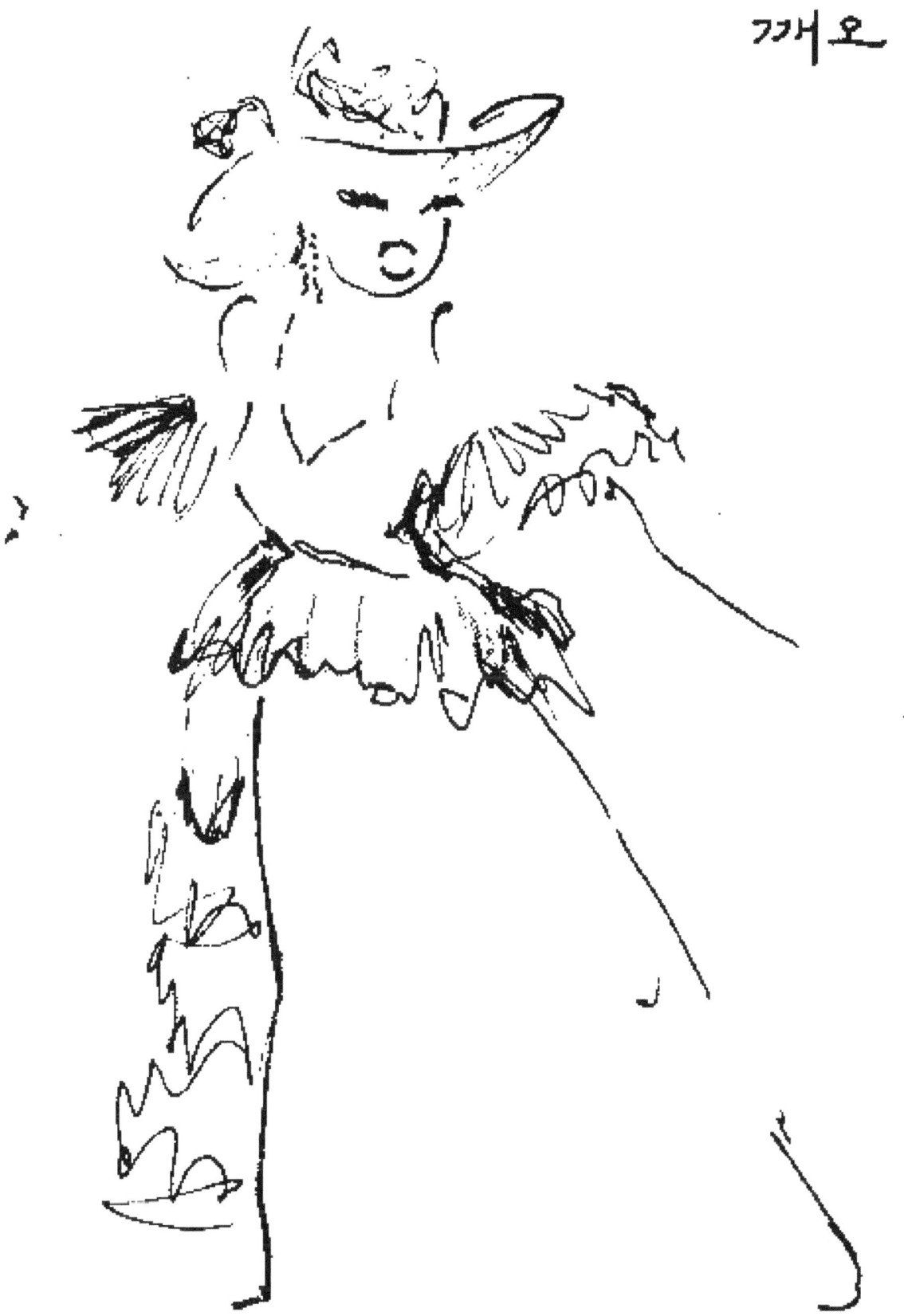

1. Use colored pencils, water-soluble is best, because when you've finished pencil-coloring, you can *-if you want to-* go back with a fine water-color paint-brush with water-damp only and play with slowly merging various patches and colors...

2. Turn off your desktop, your phone, tablet, pad and tin-can speaker-phones, so you have some actual QUIET for a few moments...

3. Go to your favorite page and start there. Go from lighter colors to darker, so you avoid muddy, brown-black finished pictures, but other than this... *anything goes!*

4. Begin coloring. Note how different strokes give you different textures. Experiment. **Play!** Pencil point size and shape also affect your picture. Up to down? Down to up? Diagonal? Fine point? Wedge-shaped? Blunt?

5. You may note after a few moments, that you're focusing on colors, light, shapes, hope, life, justice, courtesy and a host of other GOOD FEELINGS. *Enjoy.* These are your normal, natural birthright feelings, and you have every right to feel this way. When you notice you feel more creative, content, imaginative, playful or excited, REJOICE! You deserve these feelings!

Remember that coloring here, like writing a love-letter or making acoustic music or singing in a choir or growing in love, IS the payoff of the exercize and needs no permission or rationalizing.

"Art is a human act. **Art is Risky**. Generous. Courageous. Provocative. You can be perfect, or you can make art. You can keep track of what you will get in return for your effort, or you can make art. You can enjoy the status quo, or you can **make art**." Erik Wahl

For more Adult Coloring Books by Karridine, with original line-drawings from life, see the '*People Dreams*' series.

The **Cleanup Crew** Project:

RocketHub.com
http://www.rockethub.com/59614

This coloring book for adults is like many other adult coloring books that grew out of the Art Therapy movement and really became popular around 2013CE.

Created to help fund the indie film (for a possible series), this book also helps people understand some of the difficulties for people seeking racial harmony in World War II.

The **Nazi**onal Socialists (Nazis) OPENLY said that their 'white' race was a superhuman race and deserved to control, rule over and benefit from all other 'sub-humans', which included blacks, Asians, ALL-non-whites, Gypsies, Slavic, Jews, Arabic homosexual and retarded… and the list went on and on!

So '**Cleanup Crew**' pays homage to all who fought against the racist, destructive goals of the National *Socialists* and their allies.

http://www.rockethub.com/59614
Participate Today!

http://bit.ly/1HCuLk9

Find on Amazon the adult coloring book:
Cleanup Crew
for more coloring pleasure!

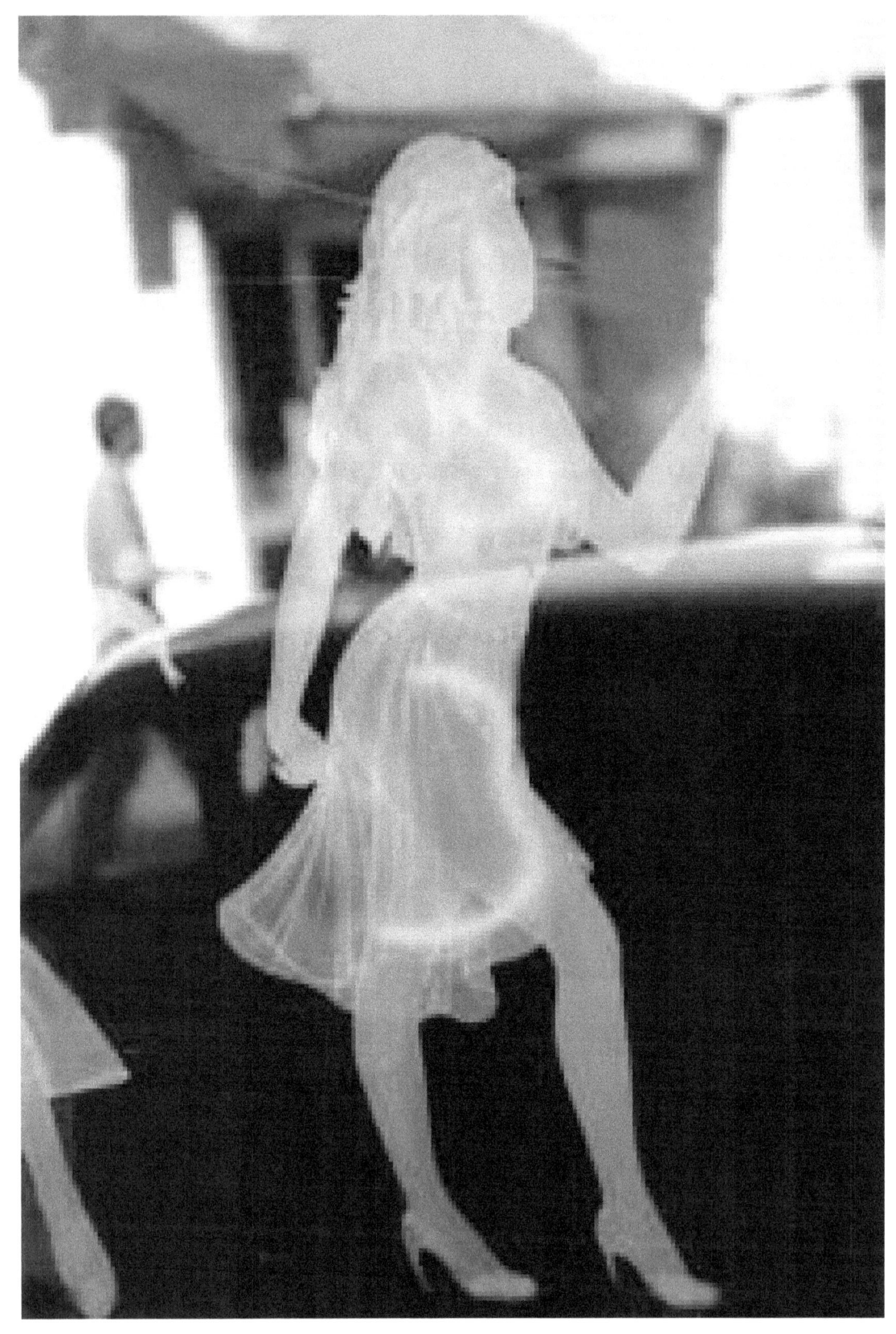

#2 of the Four Ladies, carved into 12mm plate glass
for the front of **Baby GoGo**, South Pattaya.

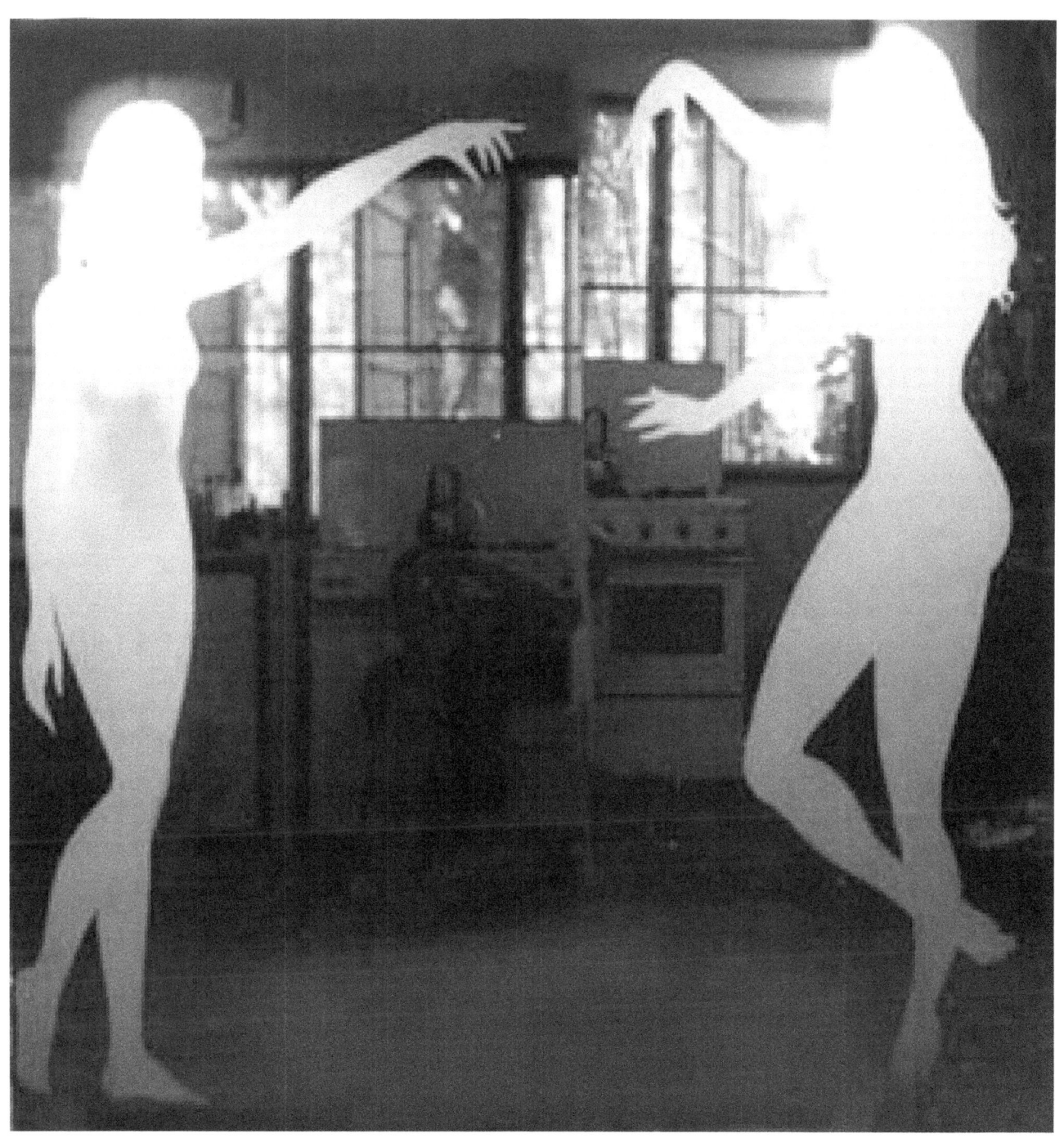

These were indoors, one for each solo-dancer stage,
and these survived longer than the Four Ladies did,
as the 'competition' was so crushed by Baby's success
that they put bricks through the Four Ladies when
they were only 5 months old...

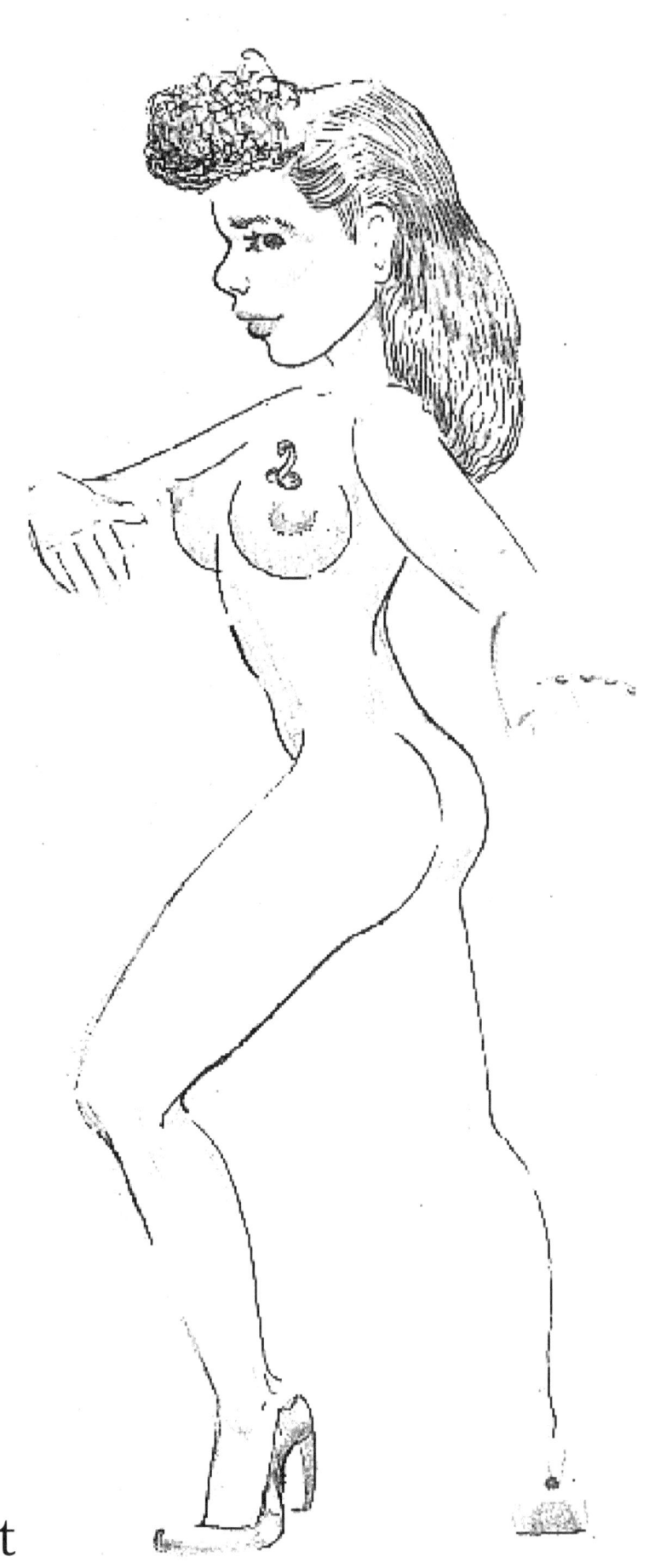

Yes, that was
a COBRA tattoo
over her heart...
Miss CobraHeart

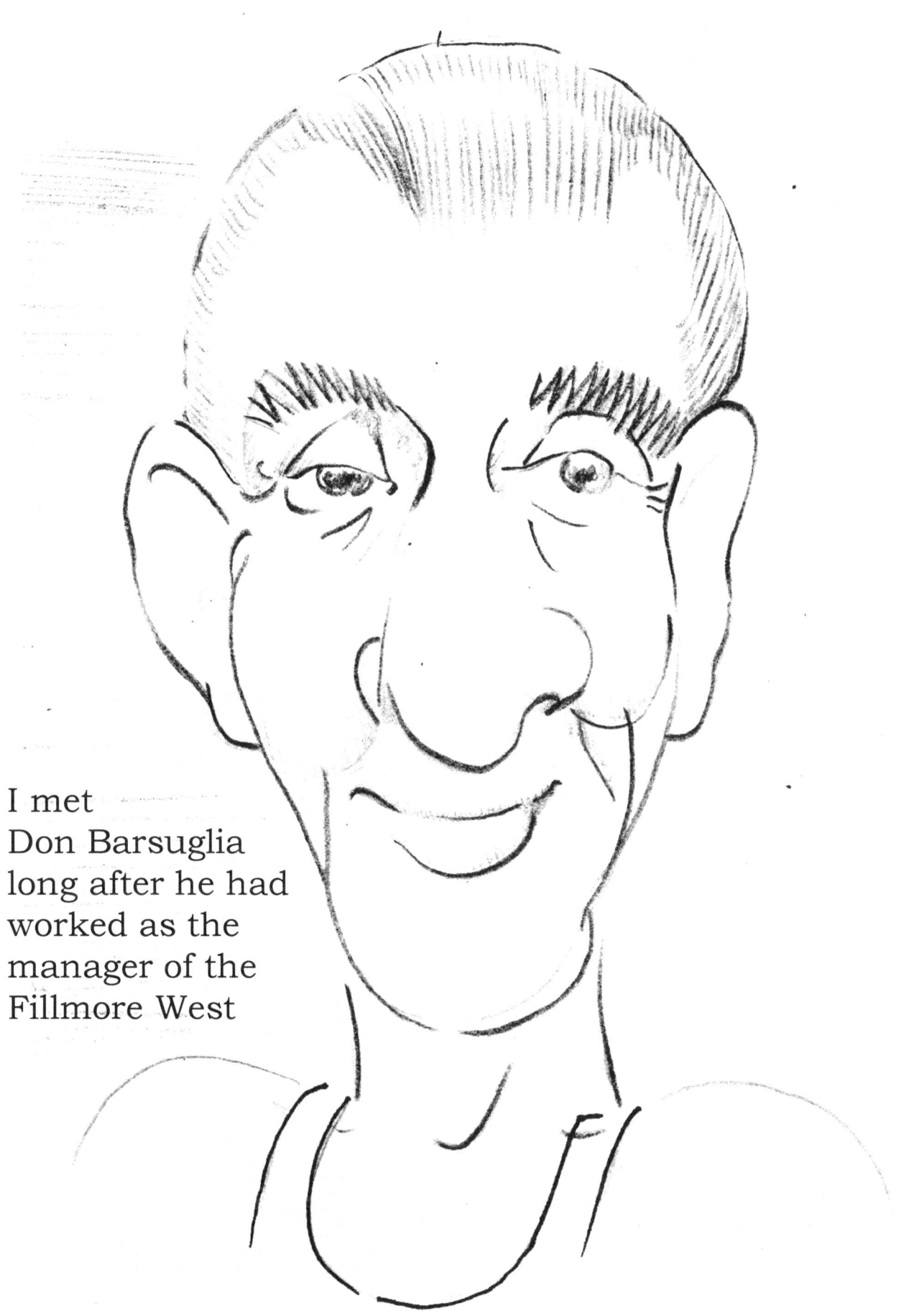

I met
Don Barsuglia
long after he had
worked as the
manager of the
Fillmore West

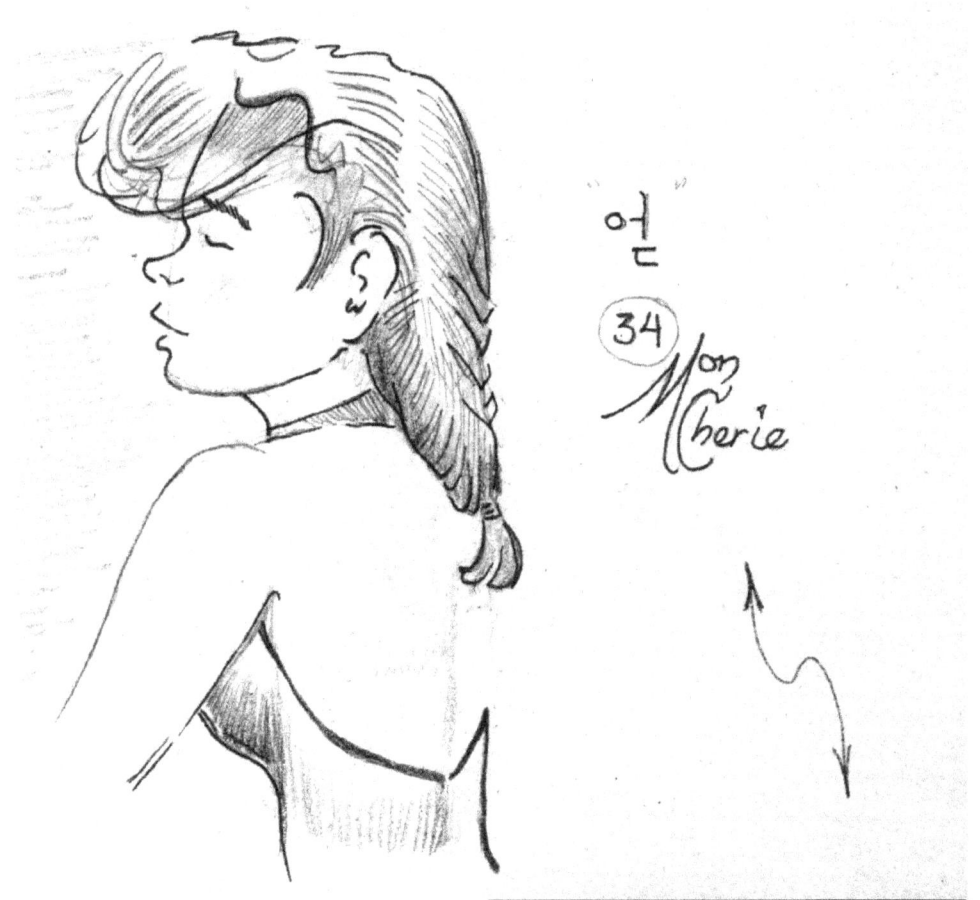

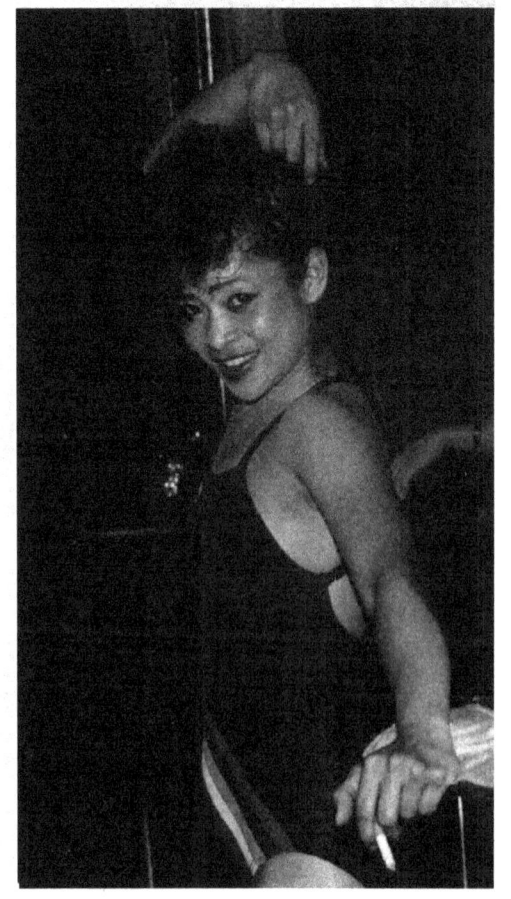

Compare
sketch with
real life...
Ohd danced
at the
Mon Cherie in
Nana Plaza

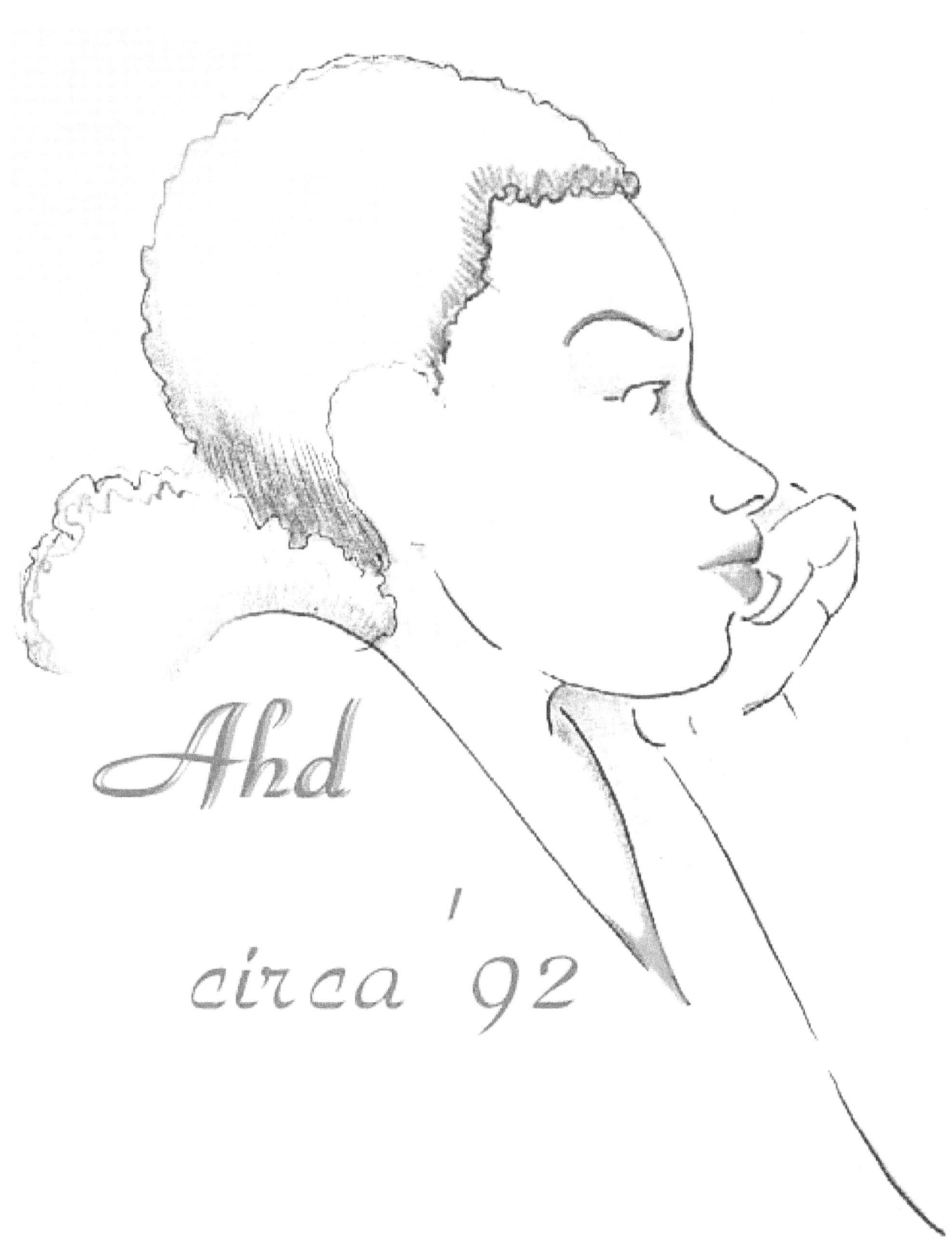

Ahd

circa '92

I loved the graceful black-Thai lines...
and her deep-red lipstick...

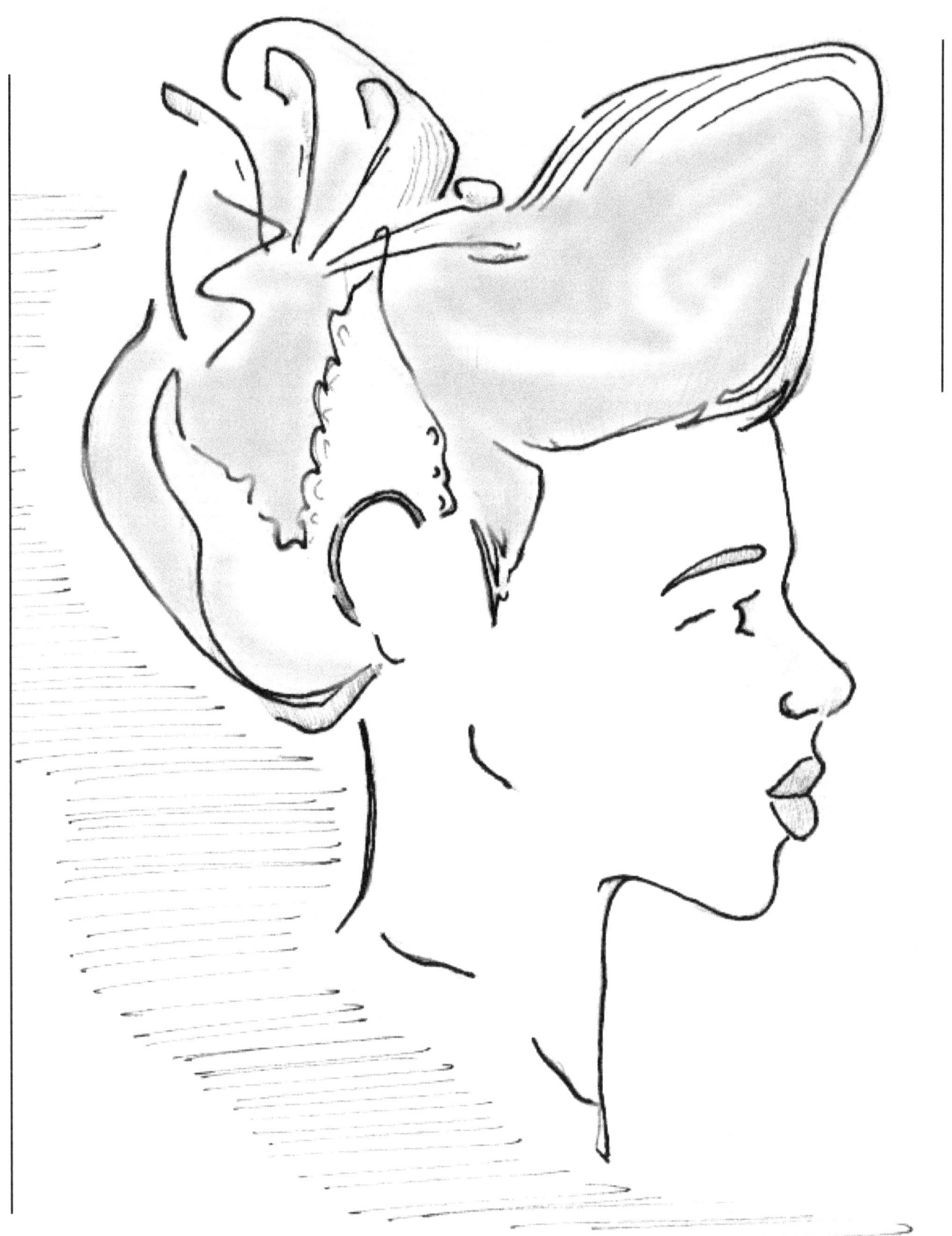

In the north-eastern plateau, historically a part of Laos and then Thailand, at any of the several holidays yearly the women wear elaborately done hair-do's...

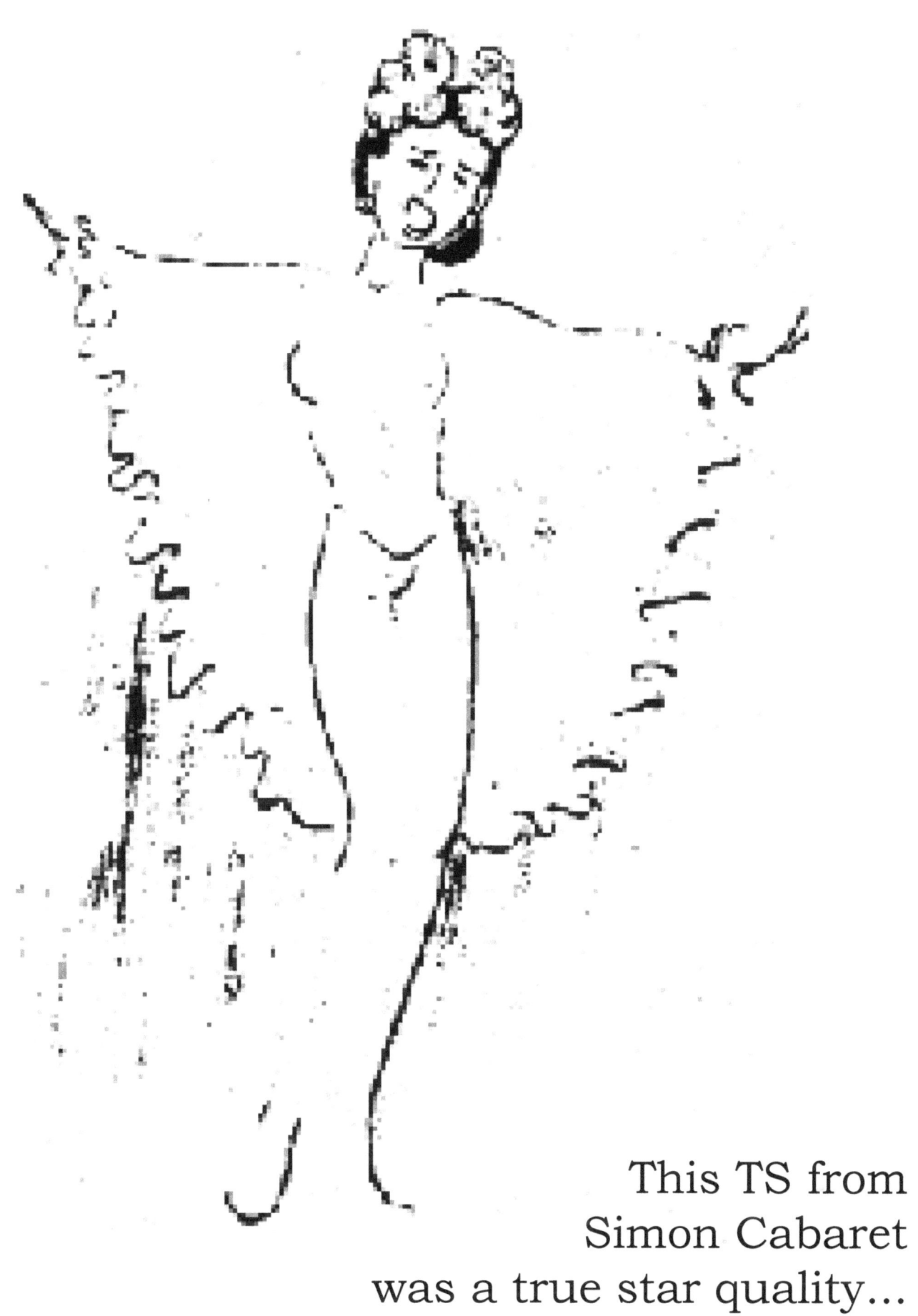

This TS from
Simon Cabaret
was a true star quality...

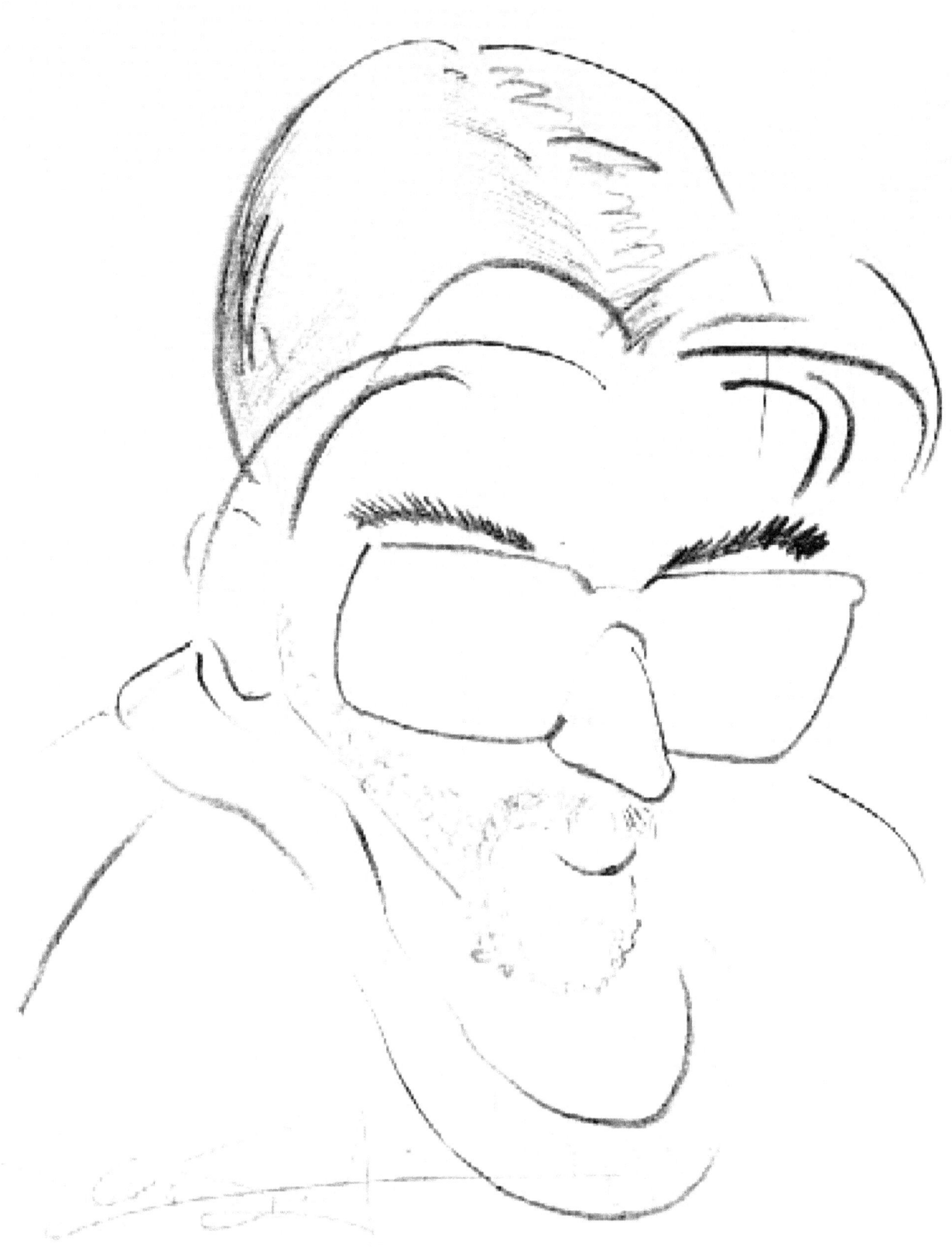

From one of the restaurant-coffee bars in Amsterdam, this sketch of The Mad Bomber... although he wasn't.

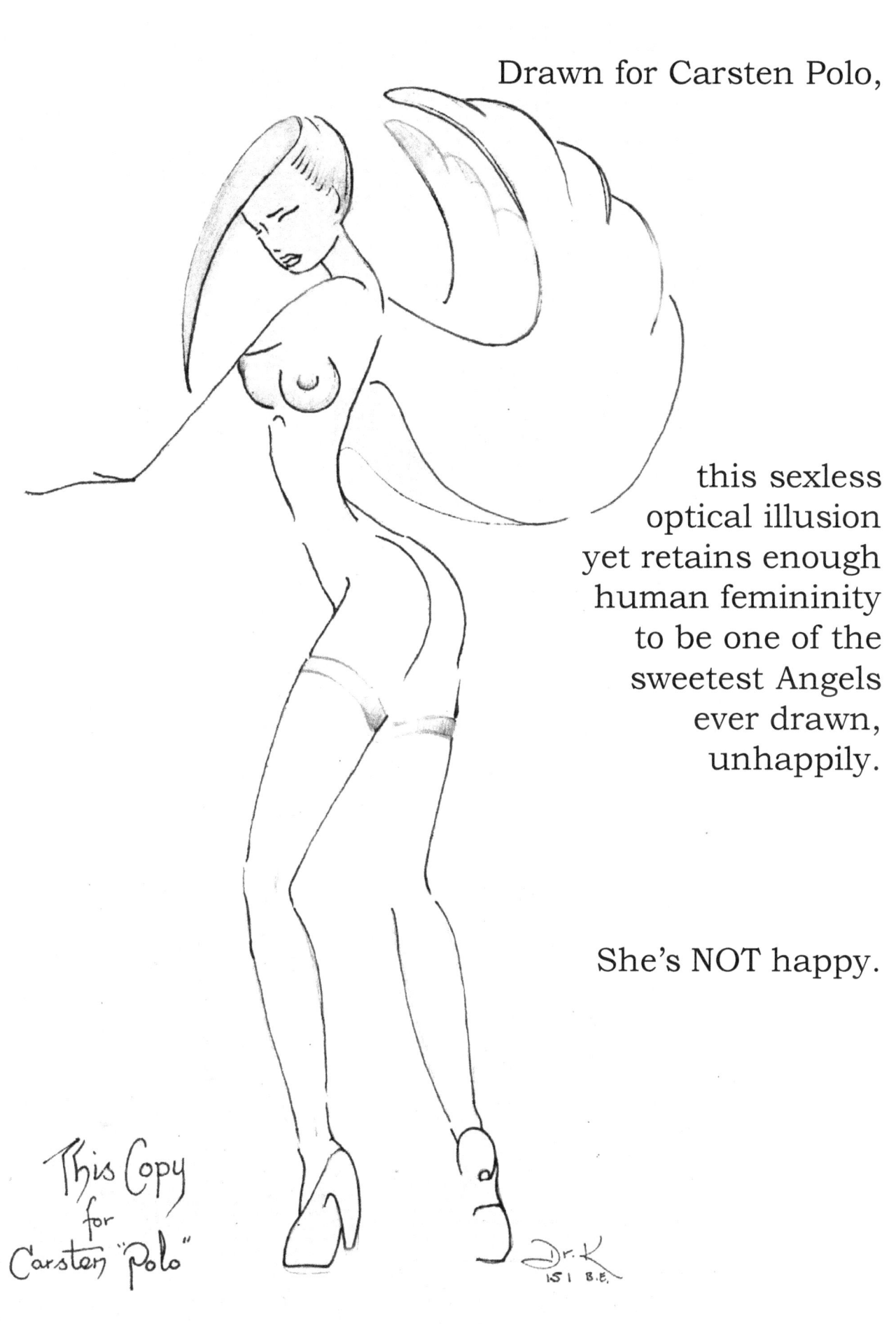

Drawn for Carsten Polo,

this sexless
optical illusion
yet retains enough
human femininity
to be one of the
sweetest Angels
ever drawn,
unhappily.

She's NOT happy.

This Copy
for
Carsten "Polo"

Dr.K
151 B.E.

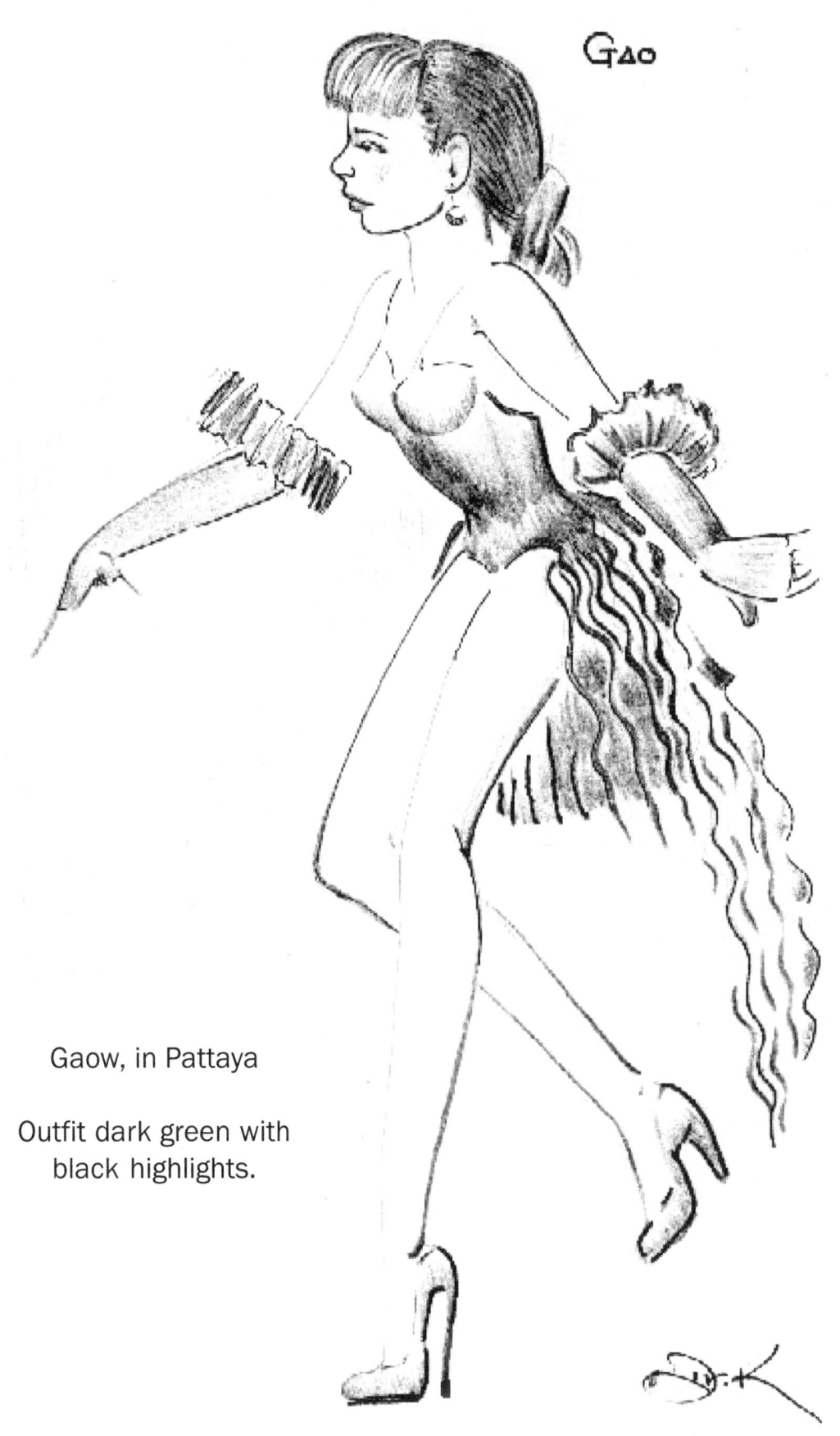

Gao

Gaow, in Pattaya

Outfit dark green with
black highlights.

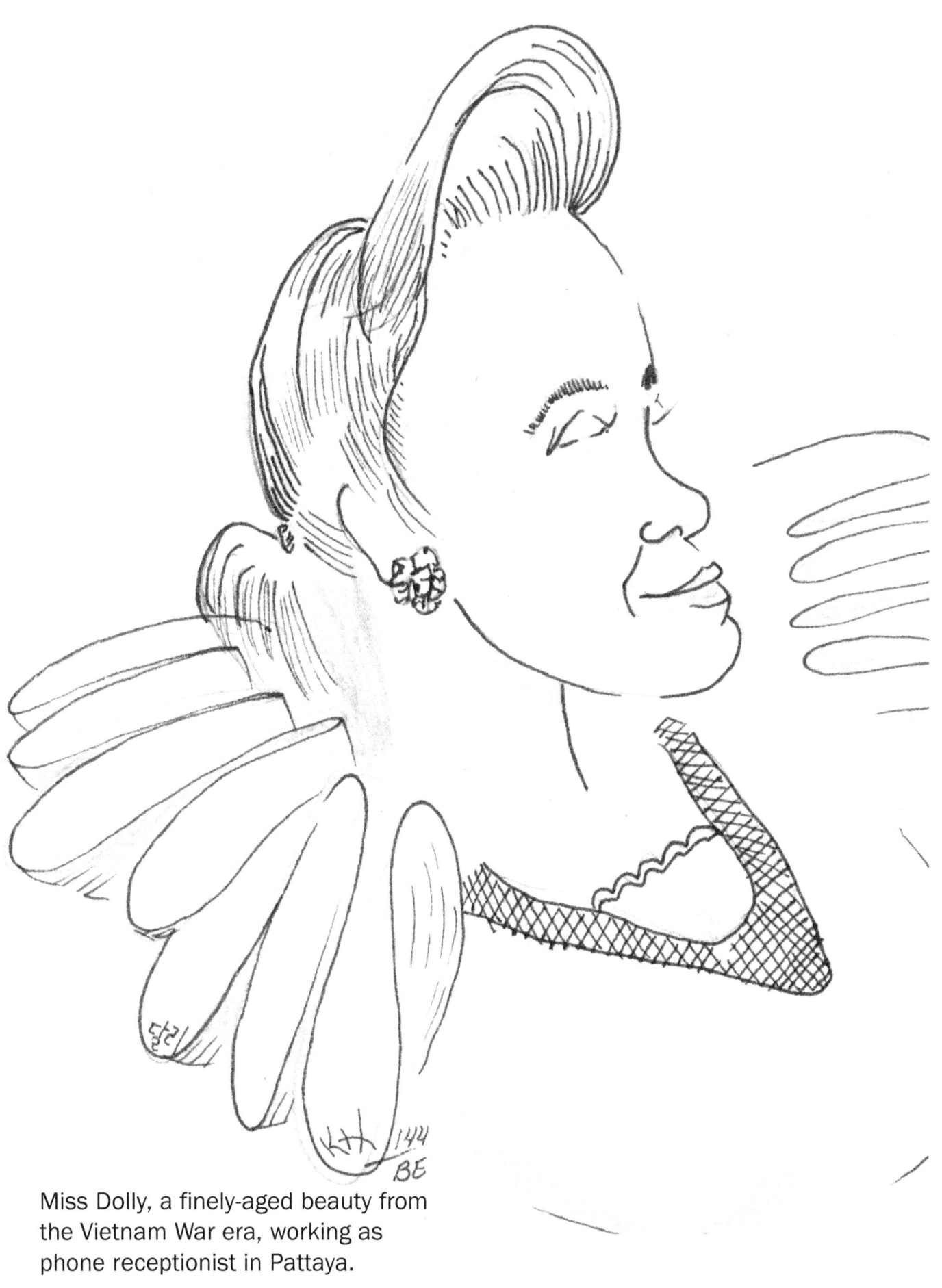

Miss Dolly, a finely-aged beauty from the Vietnam War era, working as phone receptionist in Pattaya.

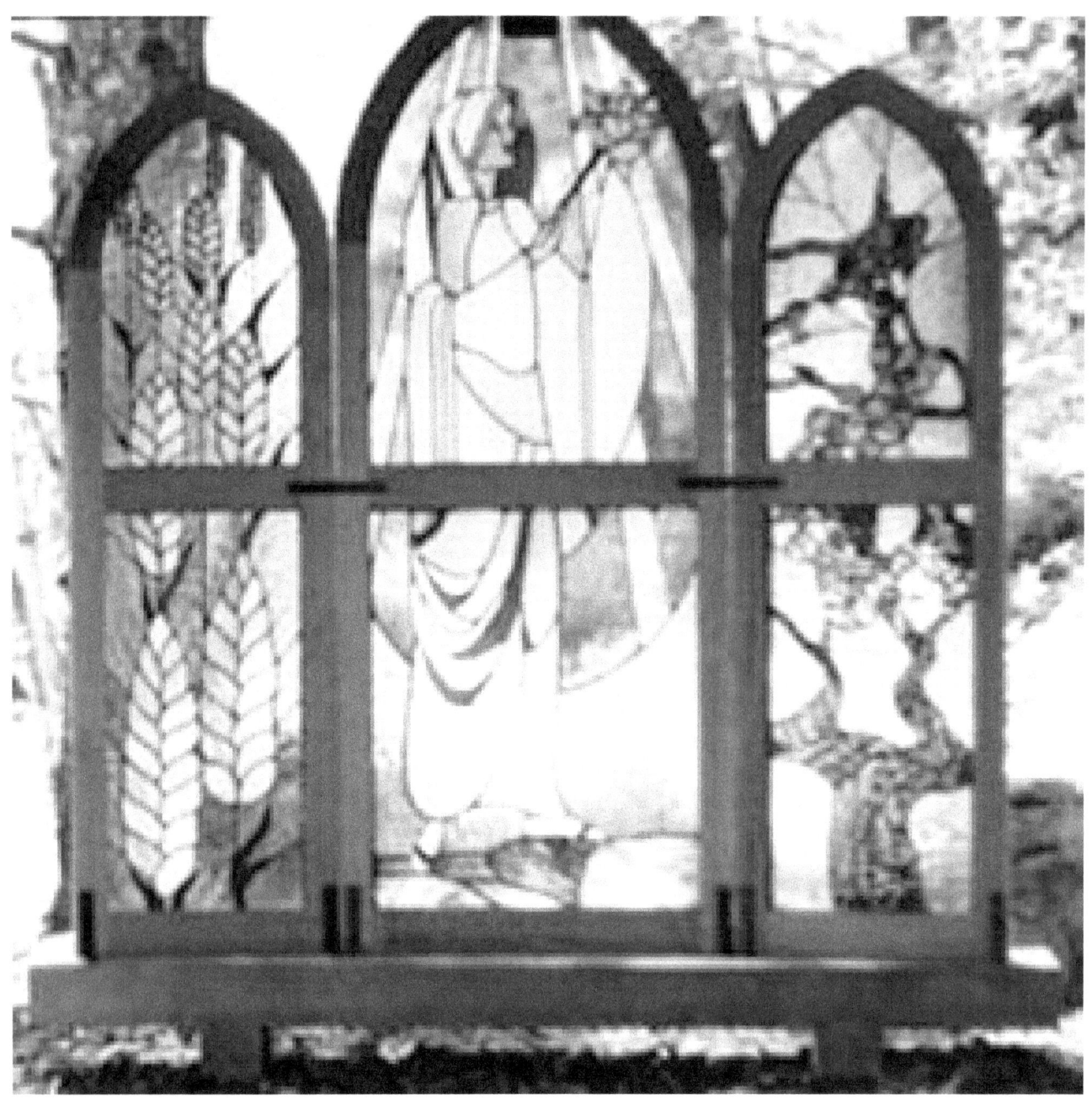

The wood frames for this stained-glass work are deep brown; the wheat on the left is light yellow-brown on a grey background. The small tree in the right panel grows from brownish-grey roots to green foliage.

The Angelic Being in the center panel wears a light-blue cloak with deep, dark-blue shadows and folds, and is surrounded by a golden-yellow radiance.
On display in northern California.

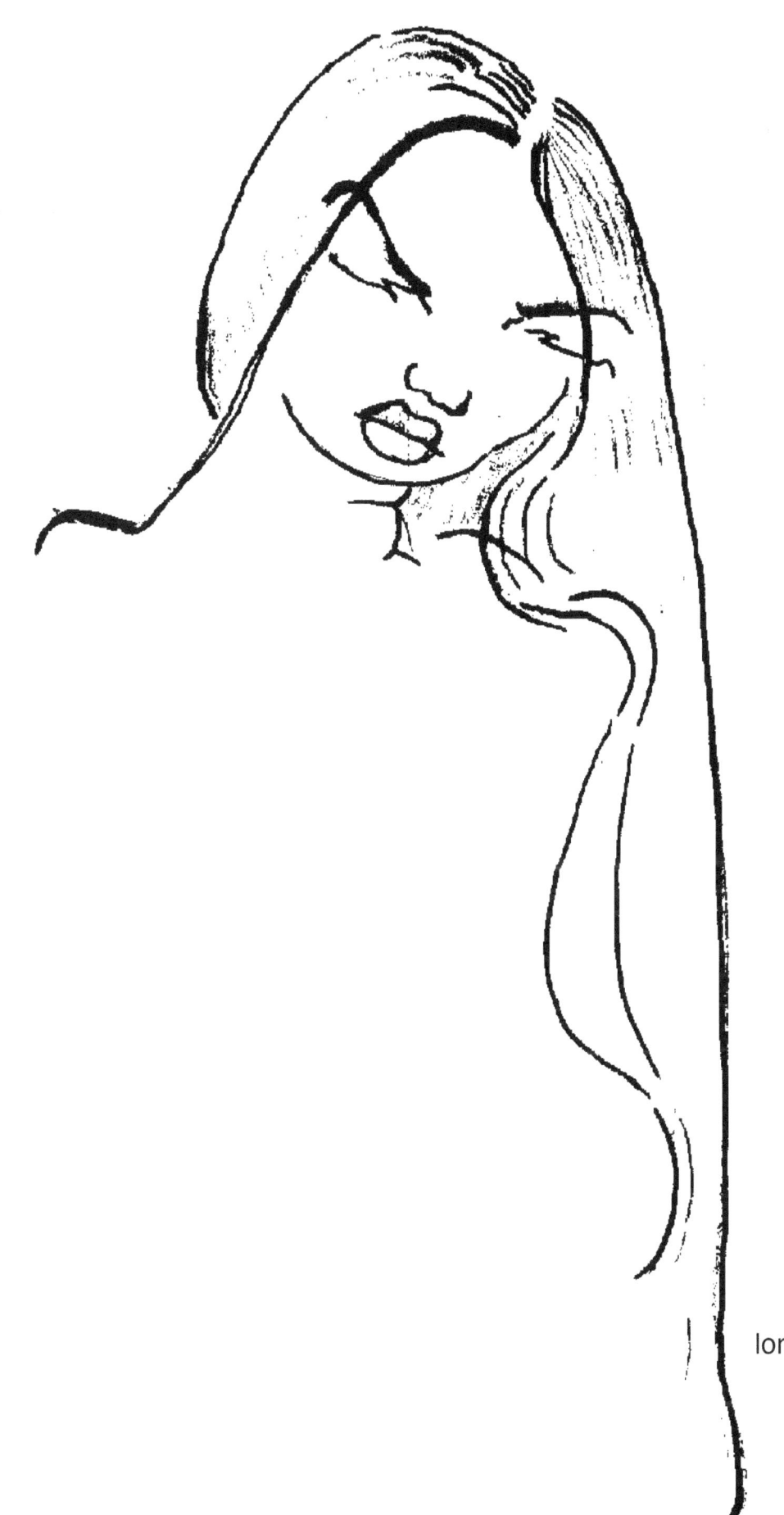

Her name is Malee
and
my designer's eye
was caught by her
long hair and lush breasts

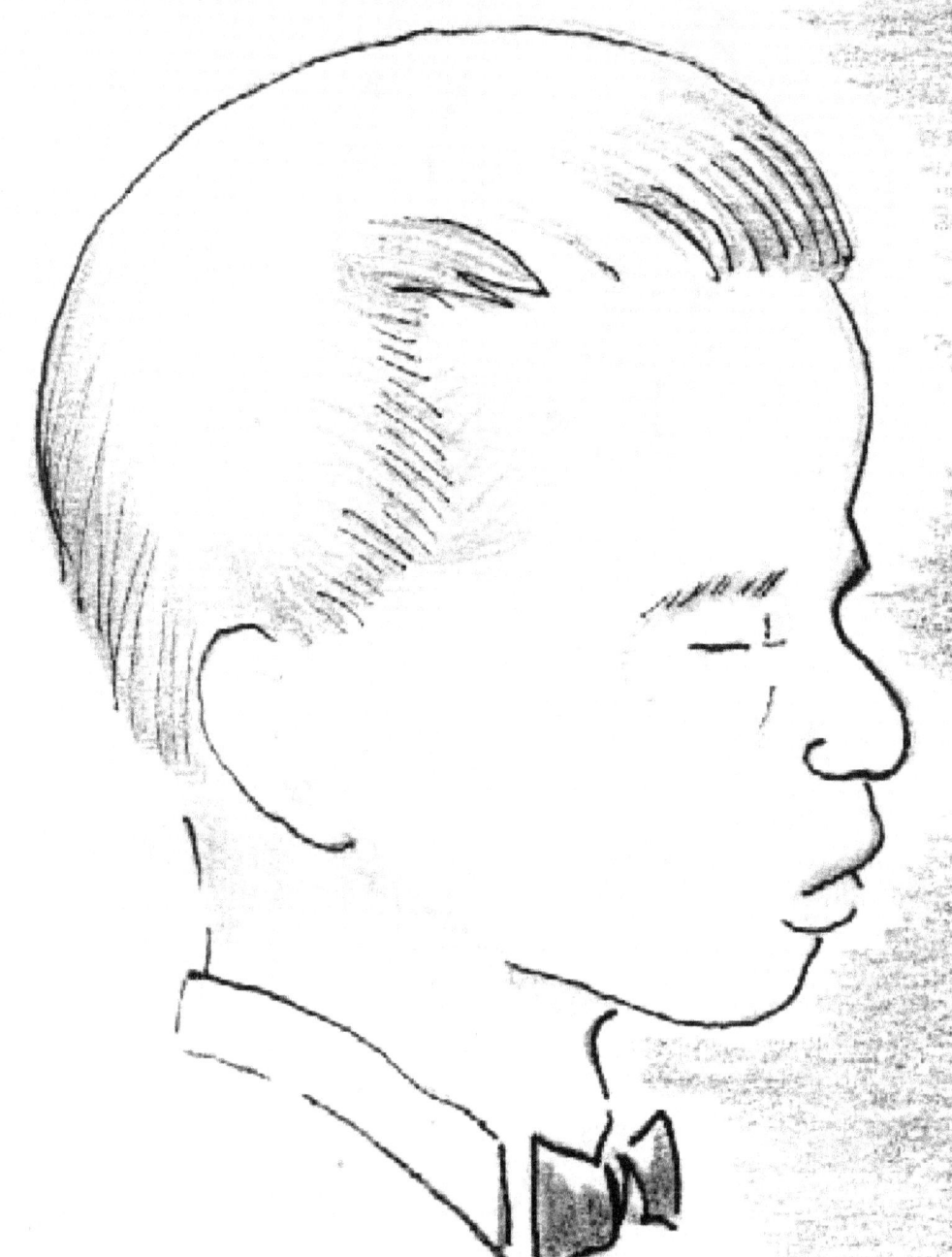

Mam Joke Moke
Bangkok, 1995

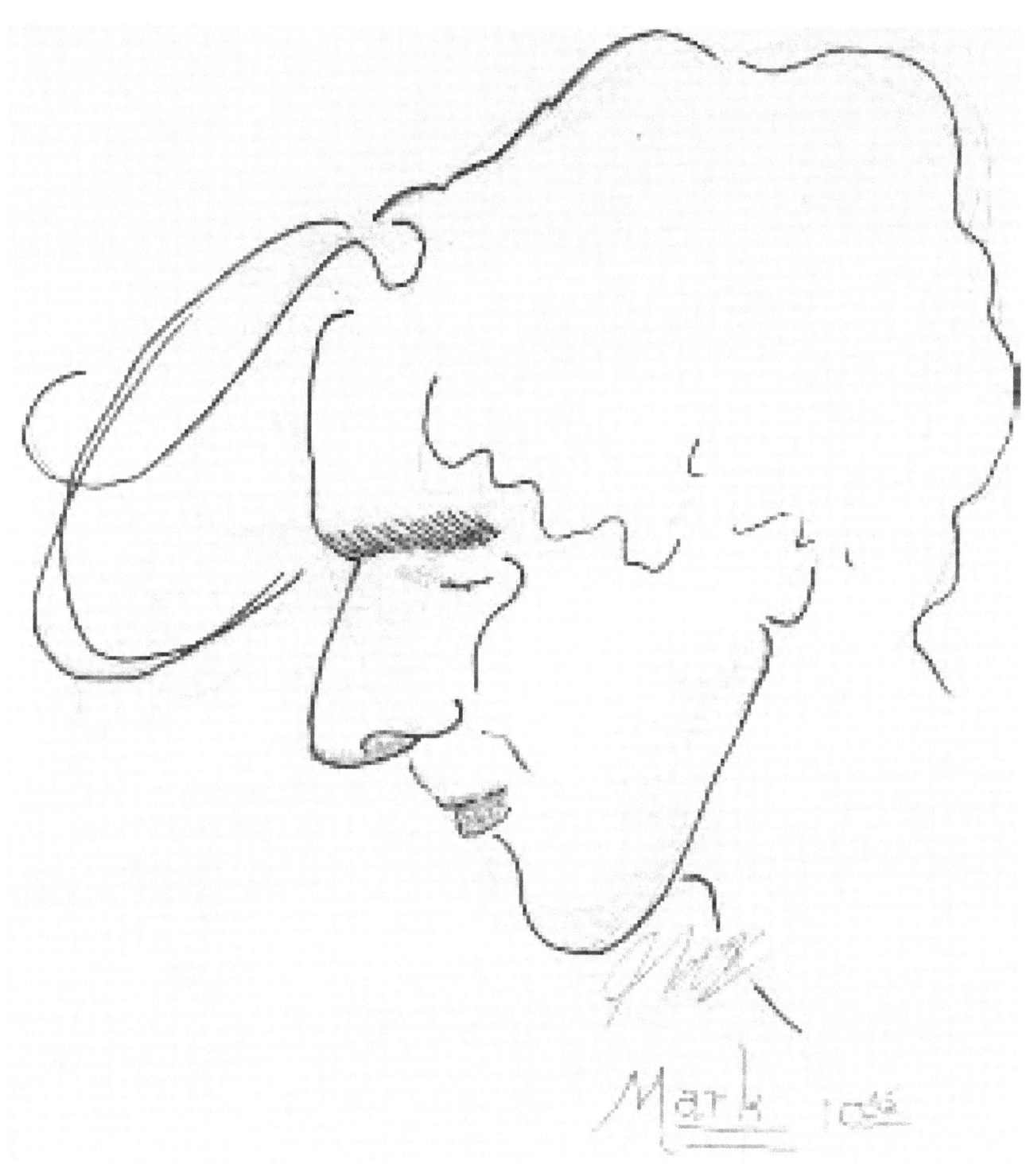

Mark, drawn on one of my rare, infrequent trips to England,
with brief stopover in Amsterdam for plane change.
Amsterdam, circa 1993
Curly brown hair, brunette beard starting to grow back...

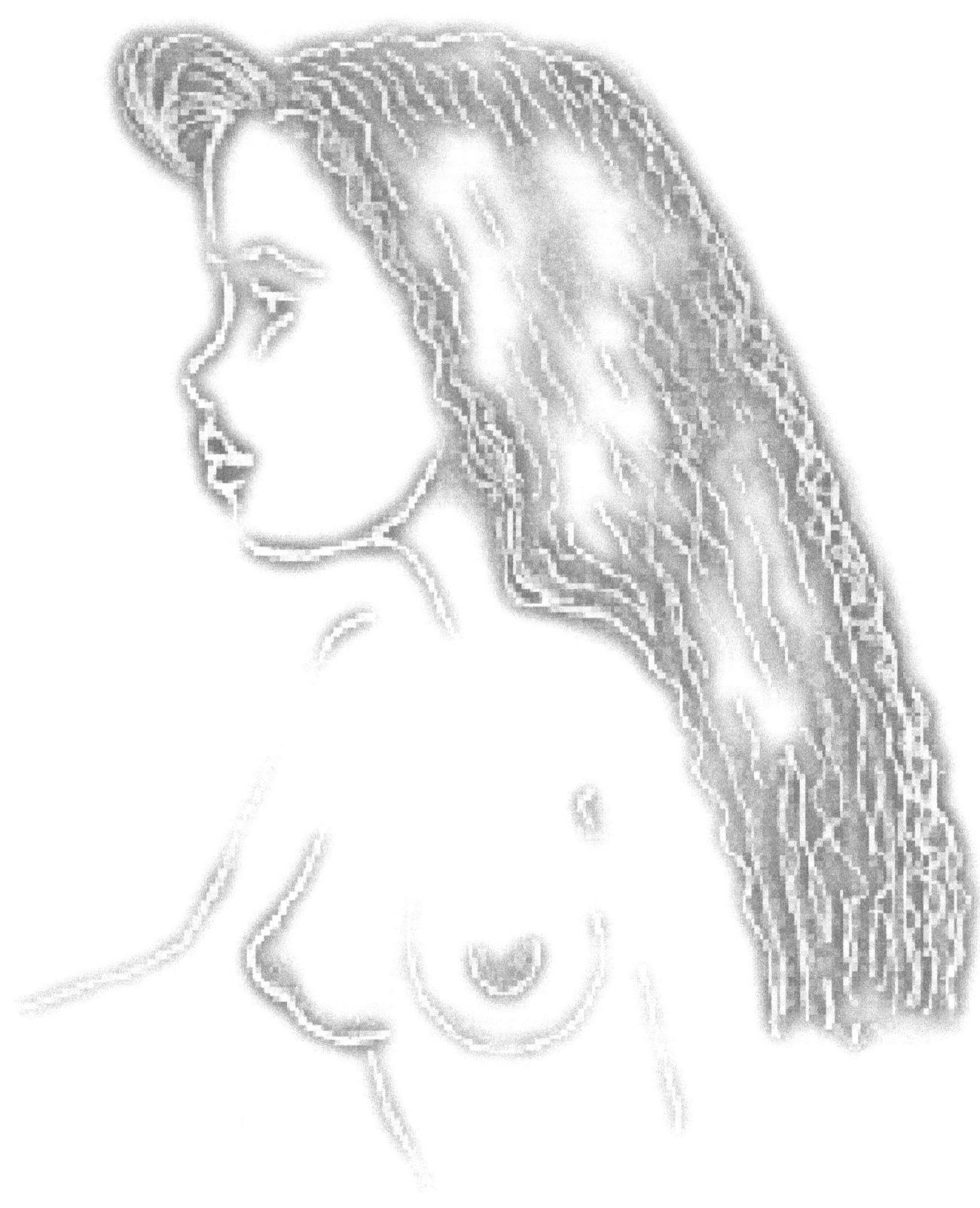

Try and get the shading and shadows right as you color this 17-18 year-old dancer from South Pattaya's '**Baby GoGo**'

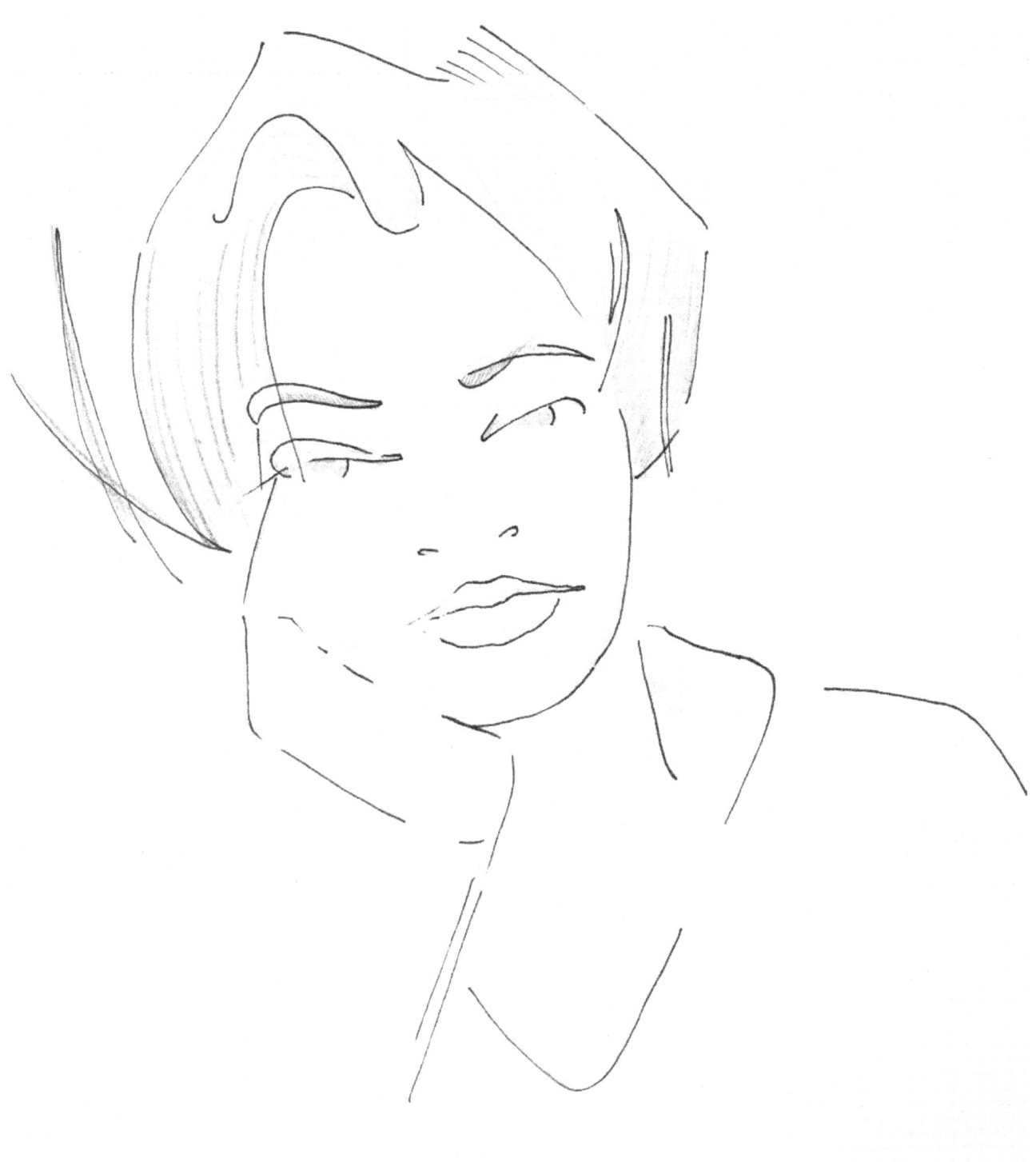

Resting her chin in her hand, Miss Hahn was a Korean student of English that wanted tutoring to improve her English, and after one of our last sessions, sat for this enigmatic caricature.

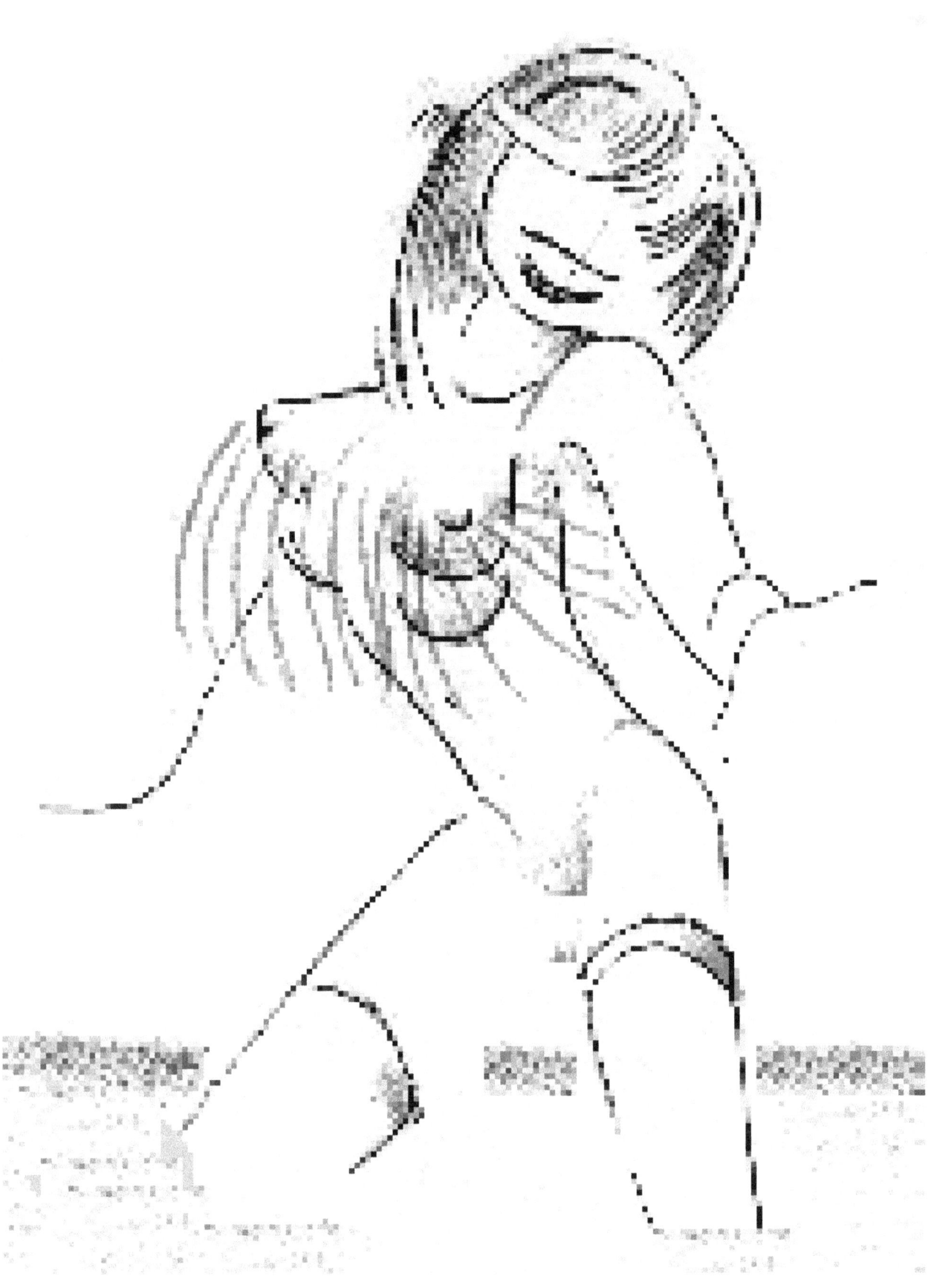

She didn't REALLY have four, I just tried to convey the energy she put into her dancing, because she was amazing!

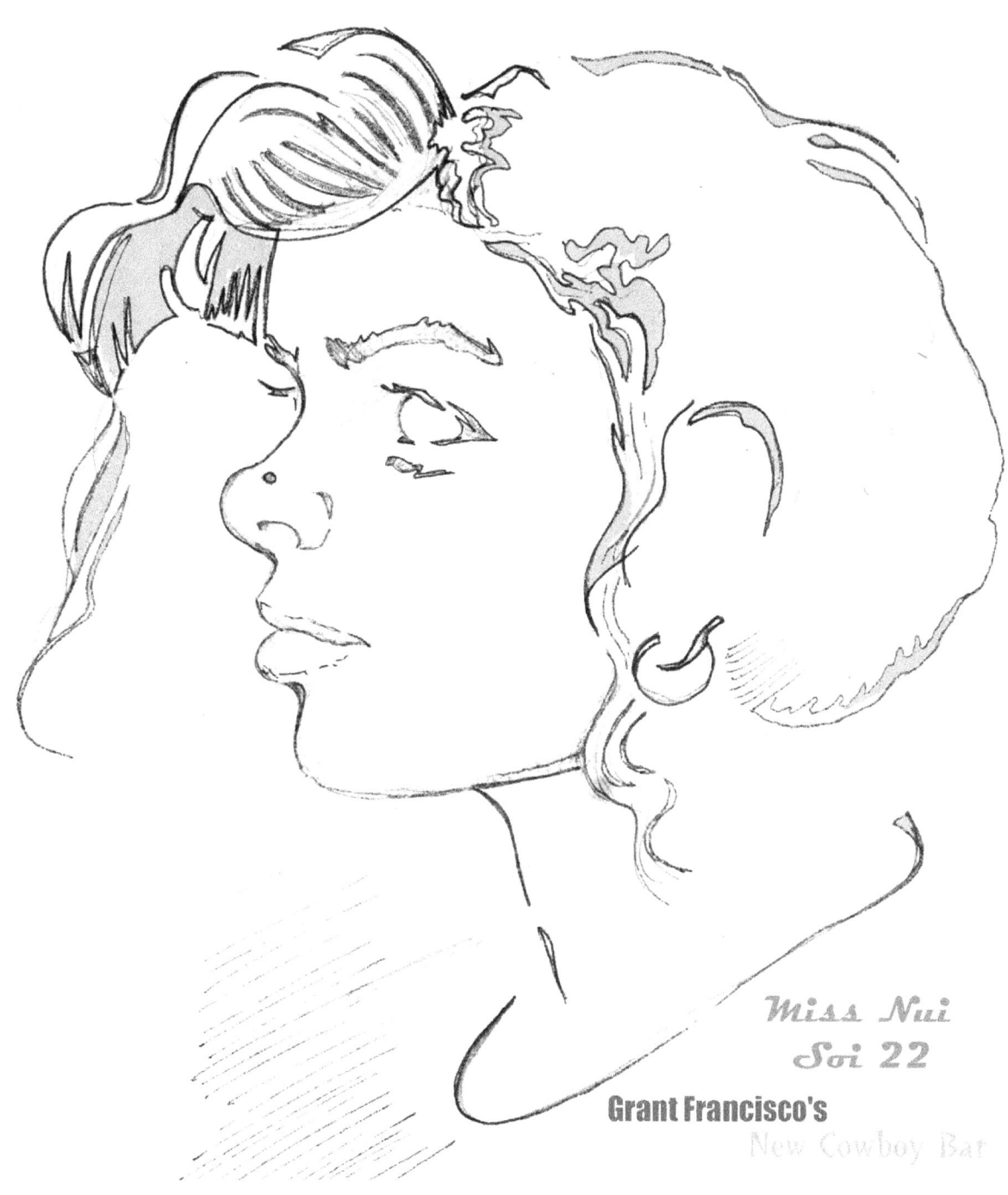

Miss Nui
Soi 22

Grant Francisco's
New Cowboy Bar

Grant Francisco moved his bar to Soi 22, off Sukumwit, and shortly thereafter died of cancer. About a year later, this young lady worked as waitress in Grant's **New Cowboy Bar**, which is there to this day (mid 2015 as we color).

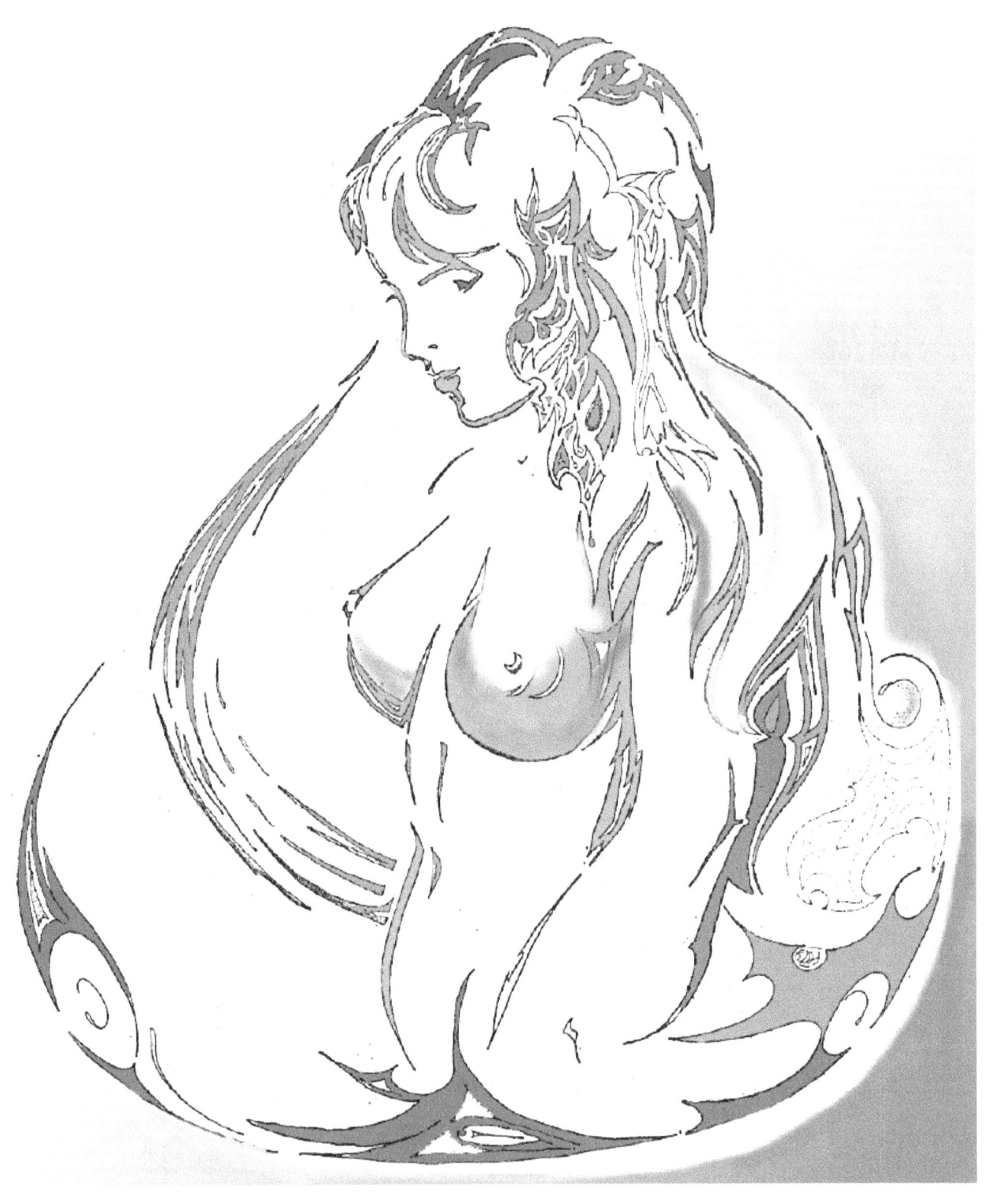

QuickSilver Girl, designed in my pre-med studies. Your choice of color themes as you fill in the nooks and crannies here... play with it, enjoy!

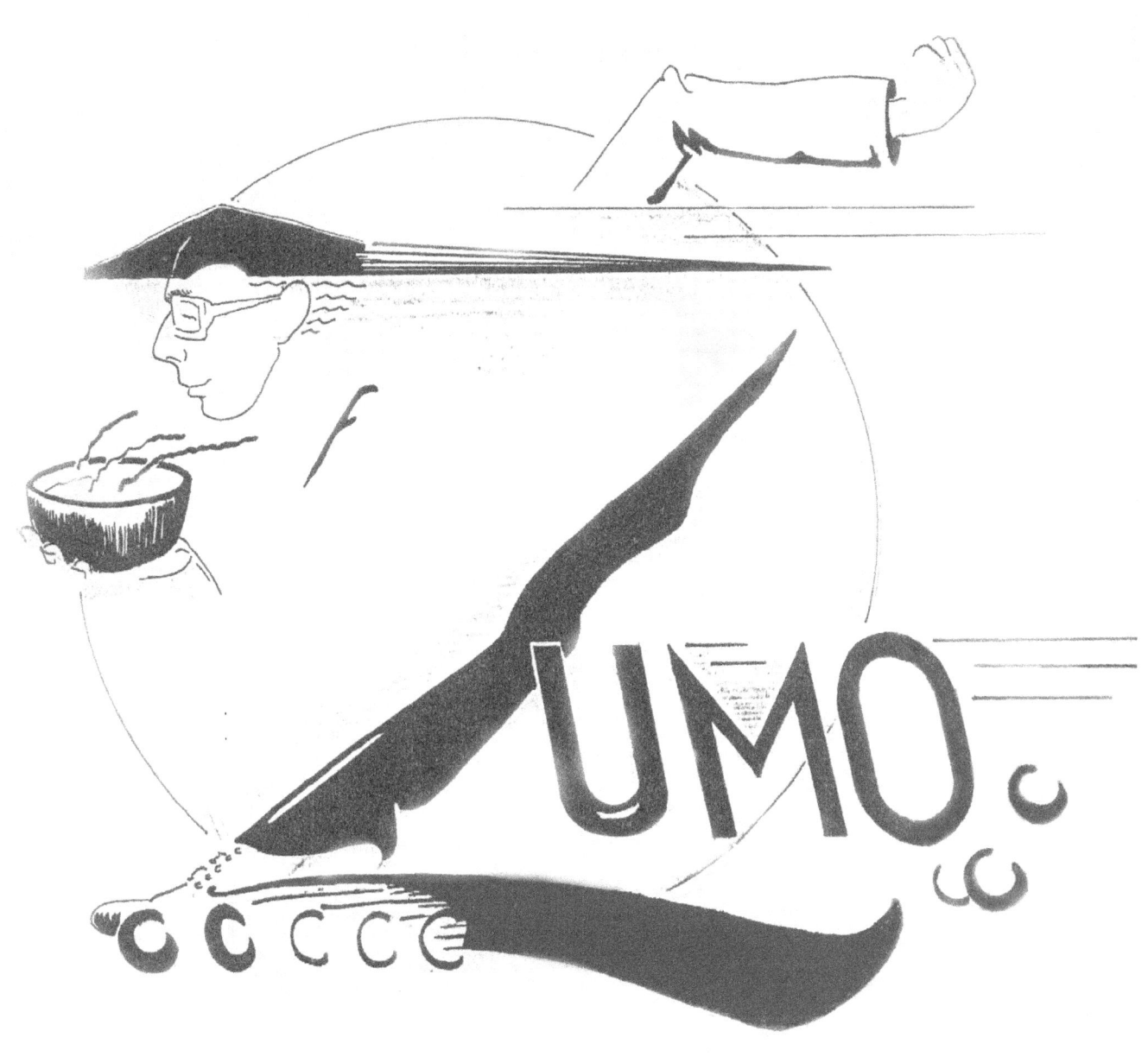

Zumo was a regular in South Pattaya for decades, on his rollerskates, zooming around delivering his DEE-Lish noodles, hot and tasty!
This was a T-Shirt concept design.

Appendix: After Words

-Miss Apple, page three, was riding her motorcycle home from work at 0330 one morning, and drove at speed into the grill of an oncoming truck. Police asked me to identify the body so they could call the family.

-**Baby GoGo** may have been Pattaya's most lucrative bar, but if so, it was in part because the owner sold SHARES at $10,000 a share; to Euro and Aussie and American investors... hundreds of them, until somebody got wise...

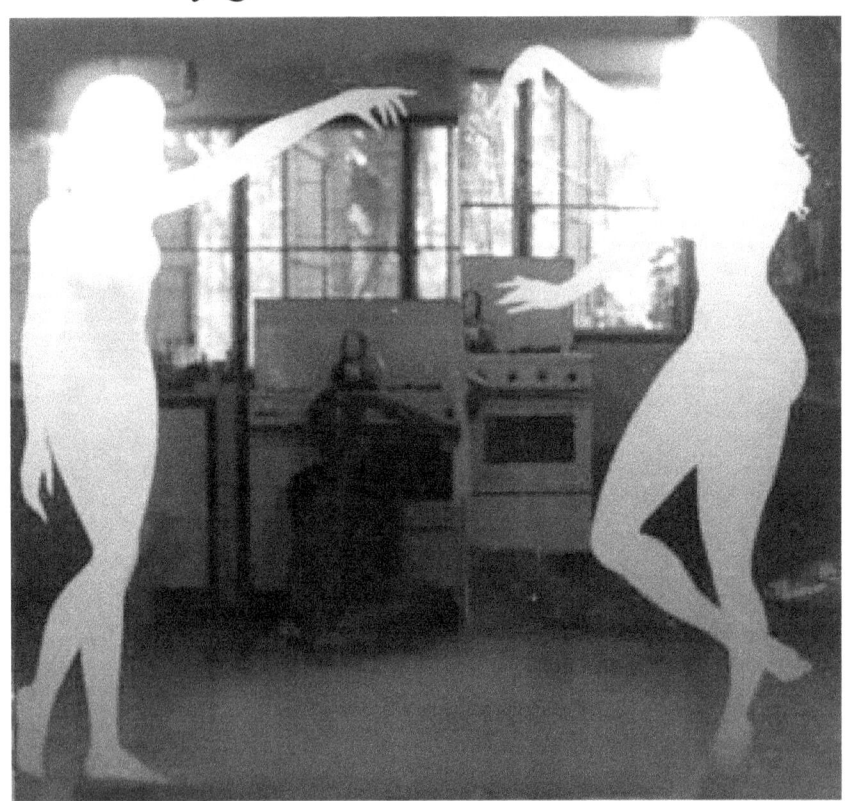

These are the mirrors I designed for Baby's interior.

+Answer to a Frequently Asked Question: No, I did NOT 'sample the delights' of the ladies drawn and sketched here..

+Yes, some are *caricatures* and some are sketch-portraits.

People Dreams #5:

Beauty by Design
Every Face a Story

An Adult Coloring Book

Not rated XXX or even PG (Parental Guidance)... this is *almost* family suitable, but since it does have a few professional dancers in various lovely stages of undress, it is probably NSFW.

So enjoy the subtle and overt pleasures of the human face and form, as you add color and details to these line-drawings; pen-and-inks, done on-location in Pattaya and Bangkok, Thailand, by artist Karridine.

These are some of the faces and forms who danced across the life-path of Karridine, and now grace the pages of this coloring book.

For further info on carved-glass custom designs, or to order your lover's portrait in glass or mirror, contact
Karridine (at) **Gmail.com**

For a chance to help make the indie film 'Cleanup Crew', go to
http://bit.ly/1HCuLk9

www.ingramcontent.com/pod-product-compliance
Lightning Source LLC
Chambersburg PA
CBHW080653180526
45168CB00008B/3406